B+T
10 ºº
2-14-75

OLIGARCHY
IN FRATERNAL
ORGANIZATIONS

OLIGARCHY
IN FRATERNAL
ORGANIZATIONS

A Study in Organizational Leadership.

ALVIN J. SCHMIDT

GALE RESEARCH COMPANY   BOOK TOWER   DETROIT, MICHIGAN 48226

Library of Congress
Cataloging in Publication Data

Schmidt, Alvin J.
      Oligarchy in fraternal organizations.

      Bibliography: p.
      1. Associations, institutions, etc.--United States.
2. Oligarchy. I. Title.
HS61.A32   366   L.C. Card No. 73-15732

To
Nicholas Babchuk
Who Motivated
Me To Study
Voluntary
Associations

ACKNOWLEDGEMENTS

The author wishes to thank a number of individuals who helped make this monograph possible.

Professor Nicholas Babchuk, under whose supervision this study initally was done as a Ph. D. thesis, was especially helpful with his comments and suggestions. As the manuscript was revised for publication, he again willingly gave of his time in reading the revised version.

The director of the Bureau of Sociological Research at the University of Nebraska, Professor Alan Booth, also deserves the author's gratitude for making himself, his staff, and the computer facilities available.

Special appreciation is extended to Mr. Keith Arrington, librarian of the Masonic Grand Lodge of Iowa, Cedar Rapids, Iowa. He and the staff were very kind and helpful in making available the library's publications and facilities. Without their assistance the present study would hardly have been accomplished.

Concerning the use of library materials, the author also wishes to thank the grand secretaries of the following fraternal and sororal organizations: the Independent Order of Odd Fellows of Nebraska, the Rebekah Assembly of Nebraska, the Knights of Pythias of Nebraska, the Pythian Sisters of Nebraska, and the Kansas Association of the Benevolent and Protective Order of Elks. A word of kindness is also extended to the Library of Congress, Washington, D.C.

Financial assistance rendered by the National Institute of Mental Health, together with the scholarship provided by the Aid Association for Lutherans, during the 1968-69 academic year, enabled the planning and execution of the research reported in this book. The University of Nebraska Graduate College Dissertation Travel Fellowship helped absorb some of the travelling expenses required to gather the necessary data.

Last but not least, the author wishes to thank his wife, Carol, and his sons, Timothy and Mark, for the many sacrifices they patiently endured while this book was written. Their patience served as a helpful stimulus.

AJS

CONTENTS

TABLES

INTRODUCTION

This monograph is a longitudinal analysis of leadership dynamics within fraternal organizations (commonly known as "lodges").[1] The issues examined in this book are drawn from the literature of formal, voluntary organizations and political sociology. Theoretical arguments from each area are empirically tested and discussed.

While the study is not directly concerned with organizational change, it does reveal findings which are relevant to that aspect of organizational theory. In this instance the reader is especially asked to note the changes that occurred with respect to leadership turnover during the first ten years as compared to the most recent ten years of the organizations' existence.

The major emphasis of the study revolves around the concept and phenomenon of "oligarchy," a word, which the author has observed, is not part of the everyday vocabulary of most people, as is the concept of "democracy." This seems strange in a country where people pride themselves of their democratic institutions. Apparently most individuals are ignorant of the fact that oligarchy is incompatible with democracy.

The concept of oligarchy, both etymologically and conceptually, like the term democracy, is of Greek derivation. Plato and Aristotle discussed the nature and characteristics of oligarchic government within the context of the city-state. Following their portrayal, oligarchy also has been discussed in other contexts. For example, Gaetano Mosca's work, *The Ruling Class,* first published in 1896, surveyed the problem of oligarchy as it applied to the Italian (national) governmental scene. Robert Michels, the German political sociologist, who formulated the famous "iron law of oligarchy," argued that oligarchic rule occurred in voluntary organizations, such as trade unions and political parties. Each viewed the phenomenon according to his *Sitz im Leben.*

Since the time of Plato and Aristotle, thousands of books and articles have been written about the nature of democracy, but relatively few have been produced that discuss oligarchy. The first definitive, theoretical account that dealt exclusively

---

[1] For reasons of convenience the term "fraternal" is employed throughout the book, even when sororal groups are part of the analysis.

with the issue of oligarchic rule was set forth by Robert Michels in 1911 when he published *Zur Soziologie Des Parteiwesens In Der Modernen Demokratie: Untersuchungen Ueber Die Oligarchischen Tendenzen Des Gruppenlebens.*[2] The English translation, which appeared in 1915, is known as *Political Parties: A Sociological Study of the Oligarchical Tendencies of Modern Democracy.* Many writers have referred to Michels' iron law of oligarchy (some only by way of a passing comment). In many instances it is quite apparent that his arguments frequently have not been read, or if read, poorly understood.

Some social scientists, for instance, Kopald (1924), Foster (1927), Garceau (1941), Barber (1948), Selznick (1949), and Harrison (1959) have published studies which essentially confirm Michels' theory of oligarchy. On the other hand, some have questioned the iron law as formulated by Michels. Gouldner, for instance, has argued: "There cannot be an iron law of oligarchy, however, unless there is iron law of democracy" (1955, p. 506). Bendix (1947) believes that an oligarchy can only occur and remain as long as a given organization is characterized by dissension. The most noteworthy publication that takes exception to Michel's law is the monograph by Lipset, Trow, and Coleman (1956), *Union Democracy.*

Sixteen statewide fraternal groups are examined in the present volume in order to test some of the theoretical statements pertaining to Michels' widely cited iron law of oligarchy. The reason for selecting fraternal groups to a large extent lies with Michels, for it was he who hypothesized that every organized collectivity was destined to become oligarchic. Thus it was reasoned, if such is true indeed, then the iron law of oligarchy also ought to be found in fraternal organizations, even though one would probably not expect these groups to be oligarchic. Why not? For one, fraternal orders place strong emphasis on emulating principles of brotherhood and democracy. Secondly, fraternal societies are primarily expressive in their activities and orientation, whereas political parties and

---

[2]Michels' first German edition appeared in 1911, not in 1913 or 1915 as some have erroneously reported. The author has a copy of the 1911 edition in his personal library.

trade-unions (groups from which Michels derived his thesis) are instrumental in scope and function. Tendencies toward oligarchy, it would seem, are more probably in instrumental organizations. The potential for effecting change in society, status of leadership, and financially rewarding salaries are significantly greater in instrumental groups than in expressive groups. Factors like these, according to Michels, are significant contributors to the formation of an oligarchy.

A third reason for selecting and analyzing fraternal groups was prompted by the fact that for generations the United States has provided the ideal government for these groups. In no other country have fraternal societies prospered more and been more prevalent than in the United States. It has been estimated that during the mid 1920s (the peak of prosperity for fraternal societies), there were some 800 different fraternal and sororal lodges (Merz, 1927). During this period about one-half of the American adult population held membership in some secret order (Schmidt and Babchuk, 1972). In the last decade or so most fraternal groups have been losing popularity and declining in memberships. Some have even gone out of existence. Nevertheless, these organizations still command the interest and devotion of millions of Americans. This being the case, it seemed very appropriate to choose fraternal orders in order to test a significant generalization such as the iron law of oligarchy.

Unlike so many studies in the social sciences, the present volume offers an analysis of longitudinal data. Such data were seen as having at least two advantages. One, oligarchy takes time to develop, and so data covering a number of years were considered very important. Two, longitudinal data were seen as capable of providing certain measures that cross-sectional information is unable to provide.

Since the concept of oligarchy has been rarely conceptualized, even in some research which purportedly has measured its presence or absence, the author shall say a few words about the present study's conceptual and operational definition of oligarchy. In attempting to follow the norm of scientifically oriented research practices, serious consideration was given to existing theoretical discussions, not to embody all previously cited aspects of the concept, but to formulate a definition that would accent the fundamental characteristics of an oligarchy: an entrenched, minority leadership. The operational definition (measure) was designed to reflect the conceptual formulation. A more comprehensive definition of the conceptual and operational aspects of oligarchy might have been desirable. The data, however, did not permit that possibility.

Finally, the author desires to say a few words about the findings reported in this volume. Although the data largely support Michels' iron law of oligarchy, they do not imply that no refinements are needed with respect to that "law." For instance, the findings in the present study relative to organizational age and size indicate that some of Michels' implicit and explicit statements require refinement, at least when applied to the fraternal organizations in the present book.

1

SOCIAL ORGANIZATION AND OLIGARCHY

In 1911 when Robert Michels, the European political sociologist, published his noteworthy work, *Political Parties,* he argued that all organizations tend to develop an oligarchic leadership. Oligarchy was the inevitable result of formal organization.

> Organization implies the tendency to oligarchy. In every organization, whether it be a political party, a professional union, or any other association of the kind, the aristocratic tendency manifests itself very clearly.
>
> . . . .
>
> With the advance of organization, democracy tends to decline.
>
> . . . .
>
> It is the organization which gives birth to the dominion of the elected over the electors, of the mandatories over the mandators, of the delegates over the delegators. Who says organization, says oligarchy (Michels, 1959, pp. 32, 33, 401).[1]

---

[1] The first sentence, "Organization implies the tendency to oligarchy," in this citation is a translation of the German: *Wer Organization sagt , sagt ohnehin Tendenz zur Oligarchie. "* This latter statement the translators translated as "Who says organization, says oligarchy" and added it to the latter part of the book, where the original edition does not contain this sentence. See Robert Michels (1911, pp. 32, 384). This observation is not intended to minimize the English translation. In fact, throughout the remaining part of the present study, whenever reference is made to Michels' work, the English edition of 1959 is cited.

Michels arrived at this conclusion by analyzing trade unions and political parties. Especially noticeable to him was the observation that in large-scale organizations[2] there were inherent elements which made genuine democratic rule, that is, control by the general or mass membership—almost impossible. "Thus the majority of human beings, in a condition of eternal tutelage, are predestined by tragic necessity to submit to the dominion of a small minority, and must be content to constitute the pedestal of an oligarchy" (Michels, 1959, p. 390).[3]

Since Michels formulated his iron law of oligarchy, numerous references have been made to it by sociologists and political scientists. Michels' law is frequently referred to when the governmental structure of organizations is discussed.

THE PREVALENCE OF OLIGARCHY

A number of scholars have supported Michels' observations by pointing to the prevalence of oligarchy. Handman (1933) and Brogan (1954), for example, see the parliamentary system of government becoming a parliamentary oligarchy through the process of cooptation, so frequently present in bureaucratic settings. Selznick says:

> Wherever there is organization, whether formally democratic or not, there is a split between the leader and the led, between the agent and the initiator. The phenomenon of abdication to bureaucratic directives in corporations, in trade unions, in parties, and in cooperatives is so widespread that it indicates a fundamental weakness of democracy (1949, p. 9).

Burnham's thinking is quite similar: "In most societies that we

---

[2]More will be said about organizational size later in the discussion.

[3]The term "oligarchy" has been given several synonyms. Garceau (1941), Barber (1948), and Truman (1951) employ the term "active minority." Sills (1968) uses the expression "minority rule." Others like Lasswell, Lerner, and Rothwell (1952) speak of "closed elites." Michael Young (1958) employs the word "meritocracy."

know about, and in all complex societies so far, there is a particular, and relatively small, group of men that controls . . . ." (1941, p. 59).

A number of scholars believe that oligarchy is found in nearly all organizations. Etzioni believes "almost all voluntary associations, effective and ineffective ones, are oligarchic" (1960, p. 267). Similarly, Burnham feels that the iron law of oligarchy holds "for all social movements and all forms of society" (1941, p. 166). And Corry says there is a "natural tendency towards oligarchy in human organization . . . ." (1947, p. 211).

Two additional references lend plausibility to the above. The National Board of the Young Women's Christian Association once complained: "There is too large an element of domination in the Association, even though that domination has on the whole expanded from being the domination of an individual to that of a small group" (Quoted in Sims, 1939, p. 222). Gist, in a historical survey of fraternal organizations, said, somewhat parenthetically, that lodges, too, develop into oligarchic structures:

> Though fraternal organizations are subject to democratic control, it appears that the actual formulation of policies, as in the case of private corporations, is largely the function of a few interested individuals, with the great bulk of the membership acquiescing so long as these policies do not interfere with their private lives (1943, p. 175).

These observations strongly support Michels' thesis. In fact, they sound remarkably similar to his bold assertion: "Who says organization, says oligarchy."

Relative to the prevalence of oligarchic structures, it needs to be noted that Lipset, Trow, and Coleman (1956) report having found an exception to Michels' model in the International Typographical Union (ITU). Although this study, *Union Democracy,* is widely cited as an exception (a "deviant case") to Michels' iron law, it can be argued that the ITU might only be an exception due to the methodology employed by the researchers. For one, the authors of that study base their conclusions on cross-sectional rather than longitudinal data. (See Chapter 5 in the present study for a more detailed discussion.)

INSTRUMENTAL AND EXPRESSIVE ORGANIZATIONS

Some of the above statements, namely, those by Etzioni (1960), Gist (1943), and Michels (1959), imply that oligarchy is prevalent, not only in "instrumental,"[4] but also in "expressive" organizations. However, the phenomenon of oligarchy has not been studied extensively and then only with respect to instrumental organizations.[5] In this context the prominent studies are as follows: Michels' (1959) treatise on trade unions, Garceau's (1941) analysis of the American Medical Association, and Lipset, Trow, and Coleman's (1956) analysis of the International Typographical Union. Very little is known about oligarchic or non-oligarchic outcome in expressive organizations.

The distinction between instrumental and expressive action or orientation in sociology was first made by Talcott Parsons (1949; 1951). He viewed instrumental action primarily as a means-end function, and expressive orientation he saw as an end in itself. Gordon and Babchuk (1959) in part adopt this distinction in their typology of voluntary associations. However, they add two additional elements: the extent to which activities of the organization are externally or internally oriented; the degree to which activities of the group provide delayed or immediate gratification. Activities of instrumental groups are externally oriented and provide gratification at a later time (after the activities in question have concluded). Expressive associations are internally directed in their activities and yield immediate gratification to its members.

Immediate personal gratification may also be obtained through fellowship and interaction with others in an instrumental organization. "This gratification, however, would be a by-product recognized by members as being separate from the organizational commitment" (Jacoby and Babchuk, 1963).

Theoretical discussions concerning the typology have re-

---

[4]Arnold M. Rose (1954, p. 52) calls "instrumental" groups "social influence" organizations.

[5]Harrison's (1959) study might be considered as an exception, i.e., if a church body is classified as an expressive organization.

ceived empirical support. Jacoby and Babchuk (1963) and Jacoby (1965) have shown that by using a series of statements representing the members' view of the organization, and by employing "judges" who rated associations by objective criteria, the instrumental-expressive dimension lends itself to empirical measurement.

Since very little is known about oligarchy in expressive organizations, the present inquiry will examine longitudinal information concerning the presence or absence of oligarchy in groups that are voluntary and primarily expressive: fraternal organizations (lodges).[6] The discussion below (Chapter 3) shows that the activities and goals of the selected fraternal groups are, for the most part, an end in themselves, immediately gratifying to the members, and internally oriented.

A second reason for focusing on expressive organizations is prompted by Michels' assertion: "The formation of oligarchies within various forms of democracy is the outcome of organic necessity, and consequently affects *every* [emphasis added] organization" (1959, pp. 401-402).

THE CONCEPT OF OLIGARCHY

Conceptualization regarding oligarchy goes back at least as far as Plato, who saw oligarchic leadership consisting of rich property owners; the poor were excluded (1935, pp. 234-332). Plato's student, Aristotle, essentially agreed with his mentor's view, except he added that the wealthy rulers were few in number. To some extent, Aristotle also saw oligarchs as corrupt, i.e., serving their self-interests (Barker, 1946).

Since Plato and Aristotle, most writers who discuss oligarchy fail to define the concept, apparently because they assume the word is understood in the light of its Greek etymology (the rule of a few).[7] Michels also fails to offer a

---

[6]That fraternal orders are primarily expressive groups is attested to by Arnold Rose (1967, pp. 223-224).

[7]See, for instance, Mosca (1939) and Pareto (1935). Neither one provides a clear conceptualization of oligarchy as they discuss the "ruling class" and the "elite", respectively.

formal definition of oligarchy, but he does link it to organization, especially size of organization: "a gigantic number of persons belonging to a unitary organization cannot do any practical work upon a system of direct discussion . . . . Hence the need for delegation . . . ." (1959, pp. 26, 27). For Cassinelli oligarchy consists of leaders who are free from membership control by virtue of an organization's large size (1953). Similarly, Presthus sees an oligarchy characterized by "the preponderance of power it enjoys" (1962, p. 40).

In the present study oligarchy is conceptualized as consisting of organizational leaders who *repeatedly succeed themselves* in one or more *executive* or *committee position* over a given number of years. This formulation goes beyond the mere "rule of the few;" it states that leaders and officials succeed themselves in one or another office within the organization; moreover, it specifies that this process continues over a number of years.

This definition of oligarchy, which focuses on leadership turnover, is consistent with Michels' *Political Parties* and with Lipset, Trow, and Coleman's *Union Democracy*, which also strongly accents leadership turnover.[8]

ORGANIZATIONAL AGE

Organizations obviously require time to develop oligarchic structures. Generalized accounts of the history of labor unions report that organizations initially show little differentiation of leaders' roles, frequent turnover of officials, and actively engaged members (Herberg, 1943). Marcus (1966) found age of unions inversely related to convention frequency (frequency of conventions was interpreted as an indication of "democracy").

---

[8]See Michels' (1959) chapter on "The Stability of Leadership." Lipset, Trow and Coleman's (1956) discussion of the International Typographical Union's two-party system, constitutional limitations on tenure of office, no loss of status upon relinquishing leadership positions, and legitimacy of party opposition really have no meaning apart from leadership turnover. In fact, the authors specifically link these characteristics to "high rate of leadership turnover" (pp. 235, 268, 446).

These observations concur with Michels' comments:

> Originally the chief is merely the servant of the mass. The organization is based upon the absolute equality of all its members . . . . In the infancy of the English labour movement, in many of the trade-unions, the delegates were appointed in rotation from among all the members, or were chosen by lot (1959, pp. 27, 28).

Scholars also note that as organizations become stabilized, membership enthusiasm and loyalty subside, creating thereby favorable conditions for an "active minority" (Toch, 1965, pp. 214-219; C. Wendell King, 1956, pp. 39-57). On the basis of this argument and the above references, it was predicted that:

(1) Organizations are less oligarchic during the early or formative years of organizational life than during later periods.

ORGANIZATIONAL SIZE

Regarding organizational size, Michels says: "as organization increases in size . . . members have to give up the idea of themselves conducting or even supervising the whole administration, and are compelled to hand these tasks over to trustworthy persons . . . ." (1959, p. 34). Lipset, Trow, and Coleman assert: "Increased size necessarily involves the delegation of political power to professional rulers and the growth of bureaucratic institutions. . . . The smaller the association or unit, the greater the membership control" (1956, p. 14). Presthus believes "the intensity of oligarchy probably increases in some sort of geometric ratio to organizational size" (1962, p. 40). Tsouderos, in a study of ten voluntary associations, found that as organizations increased in size, the membership became increasingly removed from the leadership (1955). Trade union studies reveal that large locals, compared to small ones, are less democratic. Moreover, large locals are likely to have a lower rate of turnover of union officers (Strauss and Sayles, 1953; Tannenbaum and Kahn, 1958; Strauss, 1956; Brown, 1956;

Faunce, 1962; Herberg, 1943). There is only limited evidence to the contrary.[9] Given this discussion, the study expected that:

(2)   Large-scale organizations are more oligarchic than small ones.

ORGANIZATIONAL COMPLEXITY

Conceptualization regarding organizational complexity varies with given studies.[10] However, there is one common element evident in most studies: "the degree of internal segmentation" (Hall, Haas, Johnson, 1967, p. 906).

Michels writes:

> As organization develops not only do the tasks of administration become more difficult and more complicated, but, further, its duties become enlarged and specialized to such a degree that it is no longer possible to take them all in at a single glance. . . . The rank and file must content themselves with summary reports, and . . . there is a continual increase in the number of functions withdrawn from the electoral assemblies and transferred to the executive committees (1959, pp. 33-34).

Michels' argument essentially equates organizational complexity with bureaucratization. Others, who have taken this position, have contended that bureaucracy is a type of institutional oligarchy (Duverger, 1954, p. 154). In a similar vein, Blau believes "bureaucratization blocks democratic partici-

----

[9]The findings cited as contrary to a direct correlation between organizational size and oligarchic outcome vary. Raphael in a study of unions in Cook County, Illinois, reports that the form of political organization did not vary with organizational size (1965). Another study notes that managerial succession varies directly with organizational size (Grusky, 1961).

[10]Udy (1959) portrays organizational complexity in terms of: the actual number of organizational tasks performed; the number of different tasks performed simultaneously; and the frequency of combined effort in the performance of tasks. Terrien and Mills (1955), on the other hand, see complexity in terms of administrative emphasis as measured by the number of administrators. Anderson and Warkov (1961), depict complexity in the light of structural characteristics, i.e., general hospitals are more complex than non-general hospitals. Hawley, Boland, and Boland (1965) believe "the number of departments and non-departmentalized schools" to be an index of complexity. And Hage (1965) defines complexity in the light of the number of occupations and length of training.

pation" (1956, p. 117), and Coleman says: "Bureaucratic decision-making ... occasionally does involve disregard for constitutional rights of formal democracy" (1956, p. 520). Finally Zelditch and Hopkins (1961) imply that complexity may be more critical than organizational size in affecting the structure of organizations.

In view of these arguments the following was predicted:

(3) **Complex expressive organizations are more oligarchic than those that are relatively less complex.**

SPATIAL DISTRIBUTION OF MEMBERSHIPS

The principal emphasis of this variable is on social inter-action and interpersonal communication. It is assumed that communication and social interaction are facilitated by spatial concentration of members, and that this in turn facilitates democracy rather than oligarchy. "A high degree of interaction with fellow unionists ... serves to motivate them to greater interest and participation in union politics" (Lipset, Trow, and Coleman, 1956, p. 92).[11]

Relative to why craft unions are undemocratic in large urban centers, Seidman says: "Here the workers are typically scattered among a great many employing units ...." (Quoted in Strauss, 1956, p. 535). Spinard thinks: "Where one lives (or has lived) appears to be ... associated with union participation" (1960, p. 239). More explicitly, Raphael shows local unions with spatially concentrated memberships are more likely to be democratic in structure, and locals with spatially dispersed memberships are more likely to be oligarchic (Raphael, 1965).

Inferring from these observations, it seemed appropriate to conclude that:

---

[11]Other studies that devote some attention to the variable of membership interaction are: Joseph Kovner and Herbert J. Lahne (1953), and Joel Seidman, *et al* (1958).

(4) Organizations with spatially dispersed memberships are more oligarchic than those with spatially concentrated memberships.

SPATIAL DISTRIBUTION OF MEMBERSHIPS, SIZE, AGE, AND COMPLEXITY OF ORGANIZATION

Research also indicates that spatial dispersion of membership is directly related to organizational size (Raphael, 1965, p. 281). Moreover, Raphael found, in comparing spatial dispersion with age of organization, that older unions, organized during the early period of American labor union history, "were established predominantly among persons in spatially dispersed employments" (1965, p. 278).

Spatial dispersion also seems to be related to organizational complexity. Anderson and Warkov (1961) reveal that the relative size of administrative component (complexity) increased together with the number of places at which work was performed. Similar results were found by Hall, Haas, and Johnson (1967).

Within the context of expressive associations, the present investigation hypothesized:

(5) Organizations with spatially dispersed memberships differ from those with spatially concentrated memberships in that they are (a) larger; (b) older; (c) more complex.

SUMMARY AND OUTLINE

This chapter indicated that the present inquiry was primarily prompted by three factors: 1) the wide support that numerous scholars have given to Michels' iron law of oligarchy; 2) Lipset, Trow, and Coleman's "deviant case" analysis of the ITU; 3) the absence of systematic information relative to oligarchic tendencies in expressive organizations. The chapter also introduced five hypotheses; they are as follows:

1) Organizations are less oligarchic during the early or formative years of organizational life than during later periods.

2) Large-scale organizations are more oligarchic than small ones.

3) Complex expressive organizations are more oligarchic than those that are relatively less complex.

4) Organizations with spatially dispersed memberships are more oligarchic than those with spatially concentrated memberships.

5) Organizations with spatially dispersed memberships differ from those with spatially concentrated memberships in that they are: a) larger; b) older; c) more complex.

The next chapter presents information regarding the sample of fraternal organizations that were studied; it also provides a discussion on how the theoretical concepts were measured. The third chapter depicts a brief historical background of the groups analyzed. Chapter 4 discusses and interprets the data as they apply to the tested hypotheses. The final chapter, in addition to presenting some conclusions, focuses on some implications relative to Michels' iron law of oligarchy.

2

HOW
THE
STUDY
WAS
DONE

ORGANIZATIONS STUDIED

In order to test the previously stated hypotheses, data were gathered by means of annual convention proceedings from 16 statewide fraternal groups. The following organizations were selected from Connecticut: the Ancient Free and Accepted Masons (commonly known as "Masons"), the Royal Arch Masons, the Council, the Knights Templar, and the Order of the Eastern Star. These same five orders were also selected from Nebraska. The remaining six are the Independent Order of Odd Fellows, the Rebekah Assembly, the Pythian Sisters (all three from Nebraska), the Knights of Pythias (Nebraska and Vermont), and the Benevolent and Protective Order of Elks (Kansas).

Organizations were chosen from Connecticut and Nebraska[1] in order to ascertain whether political outcome (oligarchy or

---

[1] The Elks Lodge was selected from Kansas because the Nebraska Elks did not possess complete records. Moreover, since Kansas is a contiguous state to Nebraska, it was felt no violence would be done to the industrial-agricultural dichotomy.

democracy) varies with either an industrial or agricultural region. The fact that Populism once flourished in Nebraska and Kansas might suggest that organizations in this area tend to be more democratically oriented.

CONCEPTS MEASURED

Oligarchy. In an attempt to be consistent with the conceptual definition offered in the previous chapter, this variable was operationalized by focusing on the turnover rate of the *executive officers* and *committee members* for each organization during a ten-year span. The following example illustrates how the leadership turnover rates were computed:

Following the first year of a given decade, a four-man committee, for example, had the potential of thirty-six different men holding office during the remaining nine years. Thus, if a four-man committee had nine men hold office in addition to the four that served the first year, the figure of nine men was divided by the potential figure of thirty-six yielding, in this instance, a turnover rate of 25 percent. In order to obtain one figure per organization, the mean percentage turnover rate was computed. Relatively speaking, a low turnover rate was interpreted as evidence of an oligarchic leadership.

A second measure of leadership turnover was devised, one that focused only on the percentage of leaders who had held one or more positions, either as an executive officer or committee member, for *five or more years.* This measure differs from the first index in two ways: one, its scope is more selective and restrictive in that it focuses only on leaders who have held one or more positions for *five or more years* and ignores those with less tenure; two, low percentage figures in the former measure are interpreted as oligarchic, while the latter index is seen as indicating a non-oligarchic outcome when low percentages are present.

It should be noted that it was not always possible to obtain leadership turnover rates from every committee in the sample for ten consecutive years. In some instances the committee members were either not listed every year, or the committee was not in existence for an entire decade. Thus, the data analyzed in Chapter 4 reflect turnover rates from some committees that provided rates for an uninterrupted span of less than ten years. The inclusion of these data, however, did not affect the outcome of the final results. Before the results were included from committees with less than ten consecutive years in the study, the data, relative to the mean percentage turnover rates, were compared with the results from committees that provided information for ten consecutive years. Interestingly, the mean percentage turnover rate for the first ten-year period was exactly the same for both types of committees. For the last ten years there was less than one percentage point difference between the two types of committees. In view of the nearly identical results, it was decided to include the results from committees which furnished data for less than ten consecutive years, together with the committees that revealed information for ten uninterrupted years. This was done on the basis that it presented a more complete portrait of leadership turnover.

A total of 253 committees, in addition to the executive (elected) officers of each organization, were studied during the first and most recent ten years of the 16 organizations in the sample. With the exception of three associations, which provided no consistent and reliable information on committee members for the first ten years, the number of committees studied per decade ranged from three to sixteen. The following are some of the more common committees, i.e., common to all orders, studied: Jurisprudence and Dispensations, Appeals Committee, Committee on Credentials, Bylaws Committee, Committee on Ritual, Committee on the Condition of the Order, and Resolutions Committee.

The fact that the present study examines the presence or absence of oligarchy in the light of leadership turnover rates requires a few comments. One, the writer is aware that neither the present conceptual, nor the operational definition, addresses itself to the qualitative aspect of oligarchy which some writers have seen as an important characteristic. The data do not contain any information relative to this concern. Two, the element of freedom from membership control could not be examined directly by means of the available data. However, from low turnover rates, one might infer that the rank and file not only condone low rates of turnover, but that they probably exercise little or no control over their leaders. Finally, the current investigation does not analyze a set of "conditions",[2] such as regular elections (electoral accountability),[3] wide distribution of leadership potential, referendums, appeal systems, or communication channels (e.g. organizational publications) which purportedly render organizations non-oligarchic.

While such conditions may be helpful in understanding why or how given leaders remain, or fail to remain, in office, they do *not*, on the other hand, by their mere presence necessarily indicate that an organization is therefore non-oligarchic. This contention receives support from Michels in his *Political Parties.* He notes that even regular elections are no assurance against oligarchy because members frequently re-elect incumbents out of gratitude (1959, pp. 61-62). In another context, Michels observes: "The re-election demanded by the rules becomes a pure formality" (1959, p. 100). This is supported by Prewitt's recent finding, namely, that "leadership turnover [is] not necessarily linked to election defeats. . . ." (1970, p. 14).

Regarding referendums, Michels shows that for the most part they are ineffective in preventing oligarchic outcome (Michels, 1959, pp. 333-338). And with reference to the distribution of leadership potential and skills, he asserts: "Very rarely does the struggle between the old leaders and the new end in complete defeat of the former. The result of the process is not so much a *circulation des elites* as a *reunion des elites,* an amalgam, that is to say, of two elements" (1959, p. 177). Nor is Michels convinced that channels of communication, like the organizational press and its publications, are very effective in mitigating the formation of oligarchic structures (1959, pp. 130-135).

Given these arguments, it was felt that the presence or

---

[2]Seymour M. Lipset (1954) first cited a number of such "conditions" as deterrents to oligarchy. Recently Craig and Gross (1970) examined some of these conditions.

[3]The theory of electoral accountability was first presented by Joseph A. Schumpeter (1942, pp. 269-282). Since this publication, other political theorists have seen electoral accountability mitigate oligarchic tendencies. See especially Lipset, Trow, and Coleman (1956), also Lipset (1960).

absence of an oligarchic leadership was satisfactorily assessed in the light of leadership turnover rates, especially since the turnover rates were examined for two ten-year periods, the first decade and the most recent decade of each organization.

Age of Organization. Organizational age was measured by comparing data from two time periods, i.e., the first ten years were compared to the most recent ten years of each organization in the sample. In addition, for certain purposes, it was necessary to interpret some of the data in terms of the number of years that the organizations had been in existence prior to the time of the present study.

Size of Organization. Size of organization was operationalized by taking the official membership figure for each year from the annual reports of the proceedings. From these figures the mean membership for ten years was computed, i.e., for the first ten years and the most recent decade of each organization in the sample. In order to categorize the associations into "large" and "small", the number of 10,000 members was employed as the demarcation line.[4] The smallest of the large groups had 10,181 members, and the largest of the small groups had 8,274 members.

Organizational Complexity. Complexity was operationally defined by the number of convention reports and resolutions presented to each organization's annual convention. The assumption behind this operational procedure was that complex associations require and stimulate a greater number of reports and resolutions than do less-complex organizations. In order to dichotomize the fraternal groups as "complex" and "less complex," the mean number of reports and resolutions (thirty-five) was employed.

---

[4]The figure of 10,000 is suggested by Michels (1959, p. 26); this figure is also suggested by Cassinelli (1953, p. 782).

Spatial Distribution of Members (Ecology). Since the number of chapters (subordinate lodges) per organization and their spatial distribution within the state are directly related, it was considered appropriate to measure spatial distribution of members by focusing on the number of chapters. The mean number of chapters per organization for the first and the most recent ten years was used to assign the organizations to one of two classes; those with spatially concentrated members (12 to 46 chapters), and those with spatially dispersed members (104 to 272 chapters). There were no organizations with members distributed between 47 to 103 chapters.

3

A
BRIEF
HISTORY
OF
THE
FRATERNAL
ORGANIZATIONS
STUDIED

This chapter portrays a brief historical account of the fraternal groups examined in the present study. As indicated in Chapter 2, they are the Freemasons, the Royal Arch Masons, the Council, the Knights Templar, the Order of the Eastern Star, the Odd Fellows, the Rebekah Assembly, the Knights of Pythias, the Pythian Sisters, and the Benevolent and Protective Order of Elks.

ANCIENT FREE and ACCEPTED MASONS

A brief historical sketch of each fraternal organization is best begun with the history of Freemasonry. There are two reasons for this. One, Freemasonry is the oldest of the fraternal orders in modern society. Legendary Masonry goes back to the building of King Solomon's temple when Hiram Abiff, a stone mason, supposedly chose death rather than divulge the secret masonic word (Ronayne, 1959, pp. 218-228). Darrah, a Freemason of high rank and also a scholar of the order, says many accounts that trace Freemasonry to antiquity are the result of "enchanted imagination." For instance, "Adam has been referred to as the first Mason, probably for no other reason than he wore an apron made of fig leaves" (1967, p. 20).

Freemasonry, as it is essentially known today, authentically began with the founding of the Grand Lodge of England in 1717 (Darrah, 1967, pp. 29-39). Masonry in the United States dates back to 1730 (Masonic Service Association, 1968, p.1), even though some Masonic allusions are found in the Regius or Halliwell Manuscript (a poem), reputed to be the oldest Masonic document.[1]

The second reason for first discussing Freemasonry is that, for the most part, it has served as a model for other fraternal orders. Men from the Masonic lodge frequently founded new fraternal groups, and in doing so they borrowed various elements of Freemasonry ritual and other customs. For example, Justus H. Rathbone, founder of the Knights of Pythias, borrowed ritualistic practices from the Masons (Whalen, 1966, p. 85). Masonic customs once strongly influenced the structure of the Benevolent and Protective Order of Elks when it was organized. Stevens writes: "Those who so shaped its [the Elks] destined to make it one of the leading brotherhoods . . . may be

---

[1] Some Masonic literature dates this manuscript at 926 A.D. However, Darrah says: "Experts declare it [the Regius poem] to have been written between 1427 and 1445, and from certain expressions to be a copy of one prepared about the year 1390" (1967, p. 134). The Regius poem is a small vellum manuscript, now stored in the British museum. The document stresses belief in a deity, brotherly love, honesty, secrecy, equality, etc. See Henry L. Stillson (1892, pp. 167-178) for a partial reproduction of the original manuscript.

safely classed as Freemasons . . . ." (Stevens, 1907, p. 230). The influence of Freemasonry is evident even upon cursory observation of nearly all commonly known fraternal lodges, so numerous in North America.[2] In fact, Acker refers to Masonry as "the mother of lodges" (1959, p. 14).

The term "lodge" was employed as early as 1278. It referred to

> . . . a temporary hut or shed put up near the site of a new building which served primarily as workshop, storehouse for tools, the Master's office, and so on. But it seems also to have served as a social center. Masons living away from home would eat and possibly even sleep there; meetings and discussions took place, and a certain fraternal intimacy and fellowship would be established (Hannah, 1954, p. 19).

Another common expression in Masonic literature is the term "Grand Lodge." It simply means the grand total of all lodges within a given jurisdiction. Hence, when a jurisdiction of lodges convene for annual "communication" (convention), the grand lodge is in session. The grand lodge grants dispensations to subordinate (local) lodges, and is the highest authority. In England there is one grand lodge for the entire country. In the United States each state has its own grand lodge. Thus, there is no national organization of Masons in the United States.

The name, "Freemason," which some believe was first used to designate a worker in free stone, later assumed a new significance, meaning "free of the guild" (Knoop and Jones, 1949, p. 86; Coil, 1954, p. 37). As the number of operative stonemasons declined, the number of speculative (non-operative) masons increased. In time the society became known as "Free" and "Accepted" (Darrah, 1967, pp. 90-91). Acker explains the origin of "free" and "accepted" somewhat similarly:

> In the course of time men who had no connection with the trade [stonemasons] became "accepted" members of the craft. The first known instance is that of John Boswell, who in 1600 became

---

[2]Hannah, a British authority on Freemasonry, says: "Co-Masonry flourishes in America more than in any other country. The various quasi-Masonic secret societies (Elks, Buffaloes, Knights of Pythias, Riders of the Red Robe, Ku Klux Klan, Mystic Shrine, Enchanted Realm, etc.) are, as the sands of the sea, innumerable" (1952, p. 214).

an "accepted" member of the Lodge of Edinburgh. By 1670 the "accepted" membership in the Aberdeen Lodge was in the majority, and by 1717 the "acceptance" group dominated the London lodges to such an extent that they are referred to simply as Freemasons (1959, p. 16).

The structure of Masonry consists of written laws and "landmarks" (so-called "unwritten" laws). The written laws of Masonry are the constitutions, by-laws, and general regulations adopted by the various grand lodges. Anderson's *Constitutions* published in England in 1723, six years after the formation of the Grand Lodge of England, are an example.

Landmarks must: (a) "have the character of universality;" (b) "be of higher antiquity than memory or history can reach;" (c) be "unrepealable" (Mackey, 1967, p. 3). Regarding the immutability of landmarks, the Masonic Service Association says: "no Grand Lodge can make or unmake a landmark, any more than Congress of the United States can make or unmake a law of nature" (1968, p. 3).

The number of landmarks cited by different authorities vary. Mackey lists twenty-five (1967, pp. 4-19). Darrah cites Roscoe Pound, a distinguished Masonic jurist, listing seven: "(1) belief in God; (2) belief in the persistence of personality; (3) a 'Book of the Law' as an indispensable part of the furniture of every lodge; (4) the legend of the third degree; (5) secrecy; (6) the symbolism of the operative art; and (7) that a Mason must be a man, free born, and of age" (Darrah, 1967, p. 312).

Although landmarks may vary both in number and in kind, there are some which are unequivocally accepted by all Masons. One of these is that no woman can ever become a Freemason. Even if a woman were initiated into the three degrees of Masonry by some "misguided" lodge, or by clandestine methods, she would not be regarded as a Mason.

One publication reads: "for a woman to become a Freemason is as impossible as for a man to become a mother, a leopard to change his spots" (Masonic Service Association, 1968, p. 11).

Another landmark of great importance to Masons is conducting the lodge sessions in secrecy, and having its members swear to secrecy.[3] Each of the three degrees (Entered Apprentice, Fellow Craft, and Master Mason) require extremely unconventional oaths. The oath for the first degree reads;

> Furthermore do I promise and swear, that I will not write, print, stamp, stain, hew, cut, carve, indent, paint, or engrave it [Masonic secrets] on anything moveable or immoveable ... *binding myself under no less penalty than to have my throat cut across, my tongue torn out by the roots, and my body buried in the rough sands of the sea at low water mark* [emphases not in the original], where the tide ebbs and flows twice in twenty-four hours; so help me God, and keep me steadfast in the due performance of the same (Richardson, [n.d.], p. 11; Duncan, 1968, p. 35).

In spite of the great emphasis upon secrecy, numerous books have been published on lodge rituals. Very little, if anything, really is secret if someone desires to study the rituals as a non-lodge member.[4] Gist underscores this by saying: "While it is true that chapters on ritualism contain materials which the members attempt to conceal from outsiders, the data are available to anyone who will take the time and trouble to inquire into the problem" (1940, p. 10).

Masonry asserts that it does not solicit members. "One of the fundamental concepts of Freemasonry is that application for membership must be wholly a voluntary act" (Masonic Service Association, 1968, p. 6). In the United States the

---

[3]For an interesting theoretical discussion regarding the functions of secrecy in fraternal and other secret societies see Simmel (1906).

[4]Masonry will on occasion dispute the reliability of "non-authorized" published rituals. However, Finney (1948, pp. 23-69), a former Mason, shows that the authenticity of rituals published by numerous Masons who "deviated" from the oaths is quite reliable. Some men, like Richardson ([n.d.]), for example, have made the Masonic secrets public for this reason:

> The Society of Free Masons was formed at an early age of the world, where there were no laws to protect the weak against the strong. The oaths and obligations were then undoubtedly binding, not only for the protection of the members, but for the preservation of the very imperfect arts and sciences of that period. To suppose these oaths mean anything now [about 1860] is simply absurd.

He goes on to say:

> Mankind outside a Masonic Lodge does not care a straw what takes place within that secret conclave, except as a matter of curiosity. It is partly to gratify this spirit of inquisitiveness that I have written this book, and partly to give information to Free Masons themselves. More than half the persons who join Masonic Lodges do not understand anything of the principles of the Order (p. 4).

applicant must be twenty-one years or older, and, in about half of the States (grand lodges), he must be physically and mentally sound (Masonic Service Association p. 25). Negroes and mulattoes are not permitted to join a white lodge; in fact, Negro Freemasonry (Prince Hall Masonry), which has been in existence in the United States since 1775,[5] is not recognized by most white masons in this country. Darrah says: "Regardless of the way and manner that Negro Freemasonry arose in America it is today regarded as spurious and illegitimate...." (1967, p. 323).

Before the applicant for membership is accepted a committee investigates him and reports at a regular meeting. Each applicant is voted upon by the lodge brethren. If one black ball ballot appears the vote is "foul" and a second vote is ordered by the master (head of the local lodge), because a negative vote could have occurred by mistake. However, if the second ballot again has a black ball present, the candidate is rejected for membership. This method is justified by Mackey: "Unanimity in the ballot is necessary to secure the harmony of the Lodge, which may be as seriously impaired by the admission of a candidate contrary to the wishes of one member as of three or more; for every man has his friends and his influence" (Mackey, 1967, pp. 85-87).

If the candidate is accepted, he is required to submit himself to the three-degree ritual. In addition to taking the long, unconventional oaths (mentioned above), he is stripped of his clothing, except shirt and drawers. For the Entered Apprentice degree his left breast, shoulder and arm are naked. He is hoodwinked (blindfolded) and cable-tow is placed around his neck. For the Fellow Craft degree he is again divested of his clothing; however, this time his right shoulder, arm, and breast are exposed. The cable-tow is tied around his upper right arm. The third degree, Master Mason, once more requires the candidate to disrobe. He is blindfolded for the third time, and, the cable-tow is wound around his body three times. In all three

---

[5]Negro Freemasonry came to the United States through Prince Hall who was initiated by a British army lodge group stationed in Boston. In 1784 Prince Hall and fourteen of his companions applied for a charter from the Grand Lodge of England. A charter was issued and designated as the African Lodge No. 459 with Prince Hall as Master. See Davis (1946, pp. 14-20, and Cass (1957, pp. 18-30).

instances the candidate goes through this procedure before he takes each of the three oaths. Once the Master Mason's degree is conferred, the candidate is a full-fledged member of the "Blue Lodge."

The Blue Lodge is the base or core of Masonry[6] in that two rites branch out from it: the York Rite and the Scottish Rite. A Master Mason may choose to climb either "ladder." The York Rite (of Anglo-American origin) consists of ten degrees, including those of the Blue Lodge. The Scottish Rite (of Franco-American deviation) has thirty-two degrees, also including the Blue Lodge degrees. Only thirty-second degree (Scottish Rite) and tenth degree (York Rite) members may join the Ancient Arabic Order of Nobles of the Mystic Shrine (better know as the Shriners). Although these two branches of Masonry do exist, most Masons do not "advance" beyond the Blue Lodge.[7]

The officers of a Masonic lodge, both in the subordinate (local) and the grand (state) lodge, are the Master, Senior Warden, Junior Warden, Secretary, Treasurer, Senior Deacon, Junior Deacon, Chaplain, Marshall, Stewards, and a Tyler (doorkeeper). The first five officers are elected, whereas the last six are appointed. Sometimes the Tyler,[8] however, is elected too. The grand lodge usually has several additional officers: a Sword Bearer, a Lecturer, and a Deputy Grand Master. A number of committees are appointed to carry out the organization's objectives.

Recently, American Freemasons have been experiencing a continuous decline in membership. One report to the Grand Lodge of Nebraska reads: "There are fewer petitions, more losses, more deaths, and more suspension than before. The annual gains get less and less until they are finally replaced with

---

[6]*Life* (October 8, 1956) referred to the Blue Lodge as the "core" of Freemasonry.

[7]Masonry really does not see the additional degrees above the Blue Lodge as higher degrees. One account reads: "there are no 'high degrees' or 'higher degrees.' There are only 'more degrees' than those of the Symbolic Lodges of Ancient Craft Masonry." See Masonic Service Association (1968, p. 60).

[8]The term "tyler," or "tiler," is derived from the German *"Ziegeldecker,"* meaning one who covers the roof with tiles. In Masonry the tyler closes the door and covers the "sacred" precincts from all intruders. See Mackey (1967, p. 251).

a deficit" (Wanner, 1964, p. 2).

The grand lodges in Connecticut and Nebraska clearly verify this observation. The Connecticut Masons (organized in 1789) declined from 48,095 to 44,702 members from 1958 to 1967 (a 7.1 percent loss).[9] Nebraska experienced a similar downward trend. In 1958 Nebraska had 46, 213 Masons, and by 1967 it had 43,969 (a 4.8 percent decline).

ROYAL ARCH MASONS

Although the second organization to be described is also a Masonic group, it is separately organized and operates as a distinct organization with officers, committees, and conventions. Royal Arch Masonry is frequently referred to as "Chapter" (not "Lodge") in Masonic literature (Chapman, 1892, p. 560). The Royal Arch degree (the seventh degree or four degrees after the Master Mason) appeared "some twenty or thirty years after the formation of the Grand Lodge of England. . . " (Darrah, 1967, p. 341).

Royal Arch Masonry with its four degrees is seen as a fabrication that arose out of the inventive ability of Thomas Smith Webb, an American (Darrah, 1967, p. 342). The degrees of Mark Master, Past Master, and Most Excellent Master (fourth, fifth, and sixth) "are given only under the sanction of the Royal Arch Chapter, and a Master Mason who applies for these degrees, usually enters the Chapter also, and sometimes the four degrees are given at once" (Richardson, [n.d.], p. 64).

Secrecy is stressed in the Chapter as in the Blue Lodge. The oaths for the four degrees again call forth the penalty of body mutilation. For example, the seventh (Royal Arch) degree oath in part reads: "binding myself under no less penalty, than to have my skull smote off, and my brains exposed to the scorching rays of the meridian sun, should I knowingly or

---

[9]Membership figures cited hereafter, except where noted, were obtained from the respective state organizations' (grand lodges) proceedings.

willfully violate or transgress any part of this solemn oath or obligation of a Royal Arch Mason" (Richardson, [n.d.], p. 70).

Eligibility for membership is decided by ballot, as in the Blue Lodge. All candidates must be Master Masons in good standing.

Officers in the Chapter consist of nine men: High Priest; King, or Senior Grand Warden; Scribe, or Junior Grand Warden; Captain of the Host (may act as marshall or master of ceremonies); Principal Sojourner; Royal Arch Captain; Grand Master of the Third Veil; Grand Master of the Second Veil; Grand Master of the First Veil. In addition to these, there is a secretary, a treasurer, and a tyler (Duncan, 1968, p. 219).

In the present study the Royal Arch Masons in Nebraska and Connecticut are represented. Membership in both Grand Chapters has been declining. Nebraska's membership dropped from 8,284 to 7,281 (12.1 percent) during the years 1959 to 1968. In 1955, Connecticut had 10,870 members, and in 1964 the number declined to 9,396 (13.5 percent) Royal Arch Masons.

COUNCIL OF ROYAL AND
SELECT MASTERS (THE COUNCIL)

A Royal Arch Mason may take three additional degrees (side degrees), conferred upon him by the Council of Royal and Select Masters (Mackey, 1946, II, 738). The degrees given in the Council are often known as "Cryptic degrees."

A Royal Arch Mason need not join the Council. He may go directly on to the Order of the Red Cross, Order of the Knights of Malta, and finally to the Knights Templar (discussed below), since "the Council degrees have no connection whatsoever with Ancient Craft Masonry" (Darrah, 1967, p. 344). They are "side" degrees.

The oaths are remarkably similar to those in the Blue Lodge and Chapter. The Select Master's degree, for instance, requires the candidate to swear: " . . . binding myself under no less penalty, besides all my former penalties, to have my hands chopped off at the stumps, my eyes plucked out from the sockets, my body quartered, and then thrown among the rubbish of the Temple . . . So help me God, and keep me steadfast in the same" (Richardson, [n.d.], p. 86).

The organizational structure is very similar to the Blue Lodge and the Chapter. The offices however, bear different titles. The five principal elected officers are: The Most Puissant Grand Master; Deputy Grand Master; Grand Puissant Conductor of Works; Grand Recorder; and Grand Treasurer.

In Connecticut the Council lost members. In 1955 there were 6,021 members and in 1964 there were 4,976 (a loss of 17.3 percent). Nebraska, however, had a gain of 17.5 percent. Between 1955 and 1964, its membership grew from 4,155 to 4,885.

KNIGHTS TEMPLAR

Not long after Pope Urban II had approved and proclaimed the first Crusade in 1095, there arose in 1119 a military monastic order that did not live in cloisters, but sought to protect pilgrims crusading to Jerusalem (Latourette, 1953, p. 143). Originally under Benedictine control, the Templars sson became independent and formed three classes: knights (of noble birth), who wore a red cross on a white tunic; sergeants (middle-class origin), who wore a red cross on a black tunic; the third consisted of clerics, whose duties were religious, medical and non-military (Treece, 1962, p. 137; Parker, 1963, p. 7). The Templars, who reputedly derived their name from the Temple of Solomon, where the group once had its headquarters (Fay-Cooper Cole and Warren, 1955, p. 251; C. Harold King, 1956, p. 416), grew and prospered financially as a result of their business dealings with parts of Islam.

Eventually, due to their financial success, their secret meetings, but especially their courage, the Templars became the object of suspicion and fear, which ultimately led to their demise. King Philip IV of France (reportedly denied membership in the Templars), with the help of the Pope (Clement V), succeeded, not only in condemning, but in annihilating the order by executing Jacques de Molay,[10] Grand Master of the Templars. After six years of imprisonment and torture, he was burned at the stake in 1314. With this event the once powerful order, sanctioned by the Papal office, now ironically came to a "blood-stained" end with the Pope's help (Treece, pp. 210-213.)

There are several legendary sources that seek to link the present Knights Templar to the Templars of the Middle Ages. But Darrah declares "there is absolutely nothing to show any connection whatsoever between the present Order of Knights Templar and that bank of brave men who sought to rescue the Holy Land from Moslem possession" (Darrah, 1967, p. 362). Mackey's comments are very similar (1946, II, 771). Yet, "the exploits of the old Order of Knights Templar were used as a basis [in modern Templarism] of fabricating rituals..." (Darrah, 1967, p. 364).

The origin of the modern Knights Templar (a uniformed group) has been traced to Lyons, France, in 1743 (Darrah, 1967, p. 363). The oldest American grand commandery (like a grand lodge in Blue Lodge Masonry) dates back to 1783 to South Carolina (Speed, 1892, p. 704).

The Knights Templar today is frequently referred to as "Commandery," just as Royal Arch Masonry is known as "Chapter." When three or more commanderies are instituted in a State, they form a grand commandery. The Templars also have a national organization, known as the Grand Encampment of the United States.

Local commanderies usually have twelve officers: Eminent Commander, Generalissmo, Captain-General, Prelate, Senior Warden, Junior Warden, Treasurer, Recorder, Warden, Standard-Bearer, Sword-Bearer, and Sentinel. On the grand commandery and grand encampment level the officers have the same titles, except that the term "Grand" precedes the above designations.

---

[10]The modern Masonic youth group, the Order of DeMolay, is named in honor of Jacques DeMolay.

There are three Commandery degrees: the Order of the Red Cross, Knights of Malta, and the Knights Templar. Once the Royal Arch degree has been conferred, two routes are available to become a Templar. A Royal Arch Mason may go via the Council of Royal and Select Masters, or he may go directly on to the Order of the Red Cross, Knights of Malta, and Knights Templar. The Commandery degrees are conferred by the grand encampment.

The Knights Templar are reputed to be an order for Christians only. And since "none but Christians can be admitted, consequently it cannot be considered strictly as a Masonic body," according to Mackey (1946, II, 764).

Secrecy to this order, as with other orders, is very important. Having been accepted for the tenth degree, the candidate takes a long oath, invoking corporal death upon himself should he violate any secrets or other Templar obligations. Part of the oath demands: ". . . binding myself under no less penalty than to have my head struck off and placed on the highest spire in christendom. . . ." (Richardson, [n.d.], p. 114).

The Knights Templar, in the current study, are represented by the Grand Commandaries of Connecticut and Nebraska. The Connecticut order was organized in 1827; its 1968 membership rolls had 3,100 knights. This number represented a decline of 576 (15.6 percent) since 1959. The Nebraska Templars were organized in 1817, and its 1966 membership had increased (10.8 percent) to 5,449, from 4,917 in 1957.

ORDER OF EASTERN STAR

The Order of the Eastern Star (OES), although Masonically linked, is not Freemasonry. One of the landmarks cited above clearly stated that it is impossible for a woman to be a Freemason. Thus the order is known as an "adoptive rite," even though the Masonic grand lodges exercise no direct control over the group. "A Master Mason must, however, serve as a patron of each OES chapter, and he must be present at each initiation" (Whalen, 1966, p. 26).

This female organization was established by Robert Morris, an American Mason, in 1857. He modeled the order after Freemasonry (Bell, 1956, p. 18), apparently "To give ladies a glimpse of Masonic arcana and perhaps to squelch feminine objections to lodge membership...." (Whalen, 1966, p. 25).

Membership is confined to women who are wives, mothers, daughters, widows or sisters of Masons, express a belief in a Supreme Being, and are over eighteen years of age. The order is believed to be the largest fraternal group of women in the world (Bell, 1956).

Unlike the Masonic initiation rites, the OES ritual does not require the candidate to be hoodwinked, cable-towed, or disrobed. Instead she is asked to remove her gloves, hat, and wrap. After this a thin white veil is placed over her head and face. Then she is led to the chapter room, where she is instructed and asked to take the "obligation," which pertains to secrecy, loyalty, and other elements. In comparison to the Masonic oaths, the obligations taken by the OES candidate are mild. No corporal punishment is invoked in the event a violation should result. The candidate agrees to "... maintain with vigilance the absolute secrecy to which I now assent, promising never to reveal unlawfully any of the ceremonies, signs or passes of the Order of the Eastern Star" (Bell, 1956, p. 66).

Structurally, the OES has three governing bodies: the General Grand Chapter on a national level; the Grand Chapter on the State level; and the Subordinate Chapter locally. Five subordinate chapters may unite to form a grand chapter if none exists in the State. Each subordinate chapter has the following officers: Worthy Matron, Worthy Patron, Associate Matron, Secretary, Treasurer, Conductress, and Associate Conductress. Ordinarily, these are elected. The appointed officers are: Chaplain, Marshall, Organist, Adah, Ruth, Esther, Martha, Electa, Warden, and Sentinel. They are appointed by the Worthy Matron (Bell, 1956, pp. 23-27).

The Grand Lodge of Connecticut, included in the present research, was organized in 1874. In 1967 it had 23,693 members compared to 27,823 in 1958 (a decline of 14.8 percent). The Nebraska Grand Chapter, founded in 1875, had in

1956, 44,193 members and in 1965 it had slightly decreased to 43,900 (a decrease of 0.1 percent in one decade.)

INDEPENDENT ORDER OF ODD FELLOWS

In his discussion of this order (IOOF), Whalen says: "This was the start of what is sometimes called 'poor man's Masonry' since the Odd Fellows have neither the influence, wealth, numbers, or antiquity of the Masonic Lodges" (Whalen, 1966, p. 118). This view is supported by an Odd Fellow publication: "Lodges [IOOF] were originally formed by working men for social purposes and for giving the brethren aid and to assist them in obtaining employment when out of work" *(The International Odd Fellow,* 1968, p. 7).

According to one tradition a number of London Freemasons (1830 to 1840) disagreed with their lodge, withdrew, and formed their own society, a lodge of Odd Fellows. This is thought to be the origin of the name "Odd Fellows" (Stevens, 1907, p. 247).

Wells says the first lodge of Odd Fellows was formed in 1745 in England. This lodge was the ancestor of the Manchester Unity Odd Fellows which began in 1812, in Manchester, England (Wells, 1967, IX, 812). In 1819 Thomas Wildey organized the first lodge in North America, and in 1821 the Grand Lodge of the United States was started in Baltimore, Maryland. This city still serves as the headquarters for the Sovereign Grand Lodge (national and international). In 1842 the Grand Lodge of the United States severed its ties with the Manchester Unity, with which it had become affiliated. Since that time the order has been known as the Independent Order of Odd Fellows; moreover, it declared itself "the only fountain and depository of Independent Odd-Fellowship on the globe" *(Revised Odd-Fellowship Illustrated,* 1951, p. 24). By the time Wildey died in 1861 there were over 200,000 Odd Fellows in North America (Whalen, 1966, p. 119).

Odd-Fellowship in many ways resembles Masonry. Like Freemasonry, it teaches its members secret passwords, signs, and grips; it blindfolds the candidate; it votes by ball ballot on admitting an applicant; it requires belief in a Supreme Being; it teaches certain moral lessons; and until 1971 its constitution allowed only white males to become members.

The candidate, in addition to being blindfolded, is also put into chains, symbolizing darkness and helplessness as the members form a funeral procession and then march around the lodge room. After the procession they take off the candidate's blindfold and invite him to meditate upon death as he views a human skeleton illuminated by two torches.

> As he thus realizes his own mortality, its possible nearness, and his own dependence and helplessness, he will the more willingly ponder the ties that bind him to the woes and sufferings of all around him, and joyously look forward to that bright era when all these woes and pains shall be banished by the prevalence of benevolence and peace, by the reign of brotherhood (*Revised Odd-Fellowship Illustrated,* 1951, p. 61).

In the oath or obligation the candidate promises that he "will never communicate to anyone, unless directed to do so by a legal lodge, the signs, tokens or grips, the term, traveling or other password . . . Nor . . . expose or lend any of the books or papers relating to the records or secret work of the Order...." *(Revised Odd-Fellowship Illustrated,* 1951, p. 66). The obligation further reads: "Nor will I wrong a brother or see him wronged without apprising him of approaching danger, if in my power to do so" *(Revised Odd-Fellowship Illustrated,* 1951, p. 66).

The Odd Fellows confer three additional degrees beyond the initiatory rite. They are known as Friendship, Love, and Truth, symbolized by three links joined together (the official insignia of the order).

During the anti-Masonic era (1826 to 1840) the Odd Fellows' membership suffered losses like that of the Masons. Currently the order is experiencing another noteworthy decline. Figures for Canada and the United States show that in 1958 there were 559,455 members, but in 1967 the membership list had declined to 364,843 (a loss of 34.8 percent). In the Grand Lodge of Nebraska, organized in 1858, the membership decline parallels the national decline. There were 10,754 lodge brothers in 1958, and in 1968 there were 5,987 (a loss of 44.2 percent).

THE REBEKAH ASSEMBLY

Several similarities between the Masons and the Odd Fellows were noted above. Another similarity between these two orders is that the Odd Fellows, like the Masons, have a ladies auxilliary: the Rebekah Lodge, which was organized in 1851.

Stevens says the Rebekah degree...was conferred in Odd-Fellow lodges on wives and daughters of such Odd-Fellows as had attained the Scarlet or highest degree. In 1869 separate Rebekah lodges were instituted. The requirements for eligibility to the degree have been changed several times, and in 1894 'all single white women of good moral character, over eighteen years of age,' were declared eligible, in addition to wives, widows, and daughters of Odd-Fellows (Stevens, 1907, p. 260).

All Rebekah members take one degree only. The ritual of the degree refers the candidate to "the beautiful and graceful Rebekah, whose kindness and hospitality to a humble, unknown servant, portrays grandeur of her character...." *(Revised Odd-Fellowship Illustrated,* 1951, p. 327). The reference here is to the Biblical Rebekah, Isaac's wife. The obligation a candidate takes, "without mental reservations," stresses secrecy and faithfulness to the order's laws, rules, and regulations.

The Rebekah Assembly of Nebraska, like other similar societies, is losing its sisters. In 1959 the group had 15,733 members, and in 1968 this number had decreased to 10,668 (32.1 percent). This decrease does not include the male members in the Rebekah order. The male membership for any given year comprises approximately ten percent of the female total. National membership figures show a similar trend.

KNIGHTS OF PYTHIAS

The founder of this fraternal order was Justus H. Rathbone,

a member of the Masons and the Red Men.[11] On February 19, 1864, Rathbone and several government clerks established the Knights of Pythias in Washington, D.C. In April of the same year the Grand Lodge for the District of Columbia was organized, and in 1868 the Supreme Grand Lodge of the world was formed (Valkenburg, 1887).

Rathbone once directed a school play portraying the loyal friendship between Damon and Pythias (erroneous spelling for Phintias), two Syracusans who lived during the fourth century B.C.[12] The friendship of these two men so impressed him that he "drew on this story for his ritual and borrowed elements also from some of the other lodges to which he belonged including the Masons and Red Men" (Whalen, 1966, p. 85).

Basing its ritual on the story of Damon and Pythias, this society accents the principles of Friendship, Charity, and Benevolence, In fact, the Pythian motto is: "Be Generous, Brave, and True." Pythian literature says that after the Civil War Rathbone felt the United States urgently needed these principles "to re-kindle the brotherly sentiment which had been all but stamped out under the merciless heel of human passions . . . ." *(Brief History of the Knights of Pythias,* [n.d.]).

Membership is open to any white man in good health,[13] if he accepts a Supreme Being. Black applicants were denied membership (Supreme Lodge sessions of 1869 and 1871), even before the constitution contained the "white male" clause. The Supreme Lodge constitution does now, however, contain the qualification clause. In fact, some members at the 1964

---

[11]The Red Men, or Improved Order of Red Men, is a fraternal (lodge) organization that works its degrees in American Indian dress. The order has steadily been declining in membership. See Whalen (1966, pp. 133-138).

[12]Phintias was condemned to death for opposing Dionysius, tyrant of Syracuse from 405-367 B.C. Damon offered himself as security while Phintias, his friend, went home to see his wife and child. Damon promised to die for his friend if he failed to return. The time of execution drew near, and Phintias had not made his appearance. Damon held true to his promise and permitted himself to be led to the place of execution, when suddenly Phintias rushed forward embracing his friend. Dionysius was so moved by this incident that he released both and asked to join their friendship. For a full account see: P.C. Kibbe (1930).

[13]In 1870 the order did not admit maimed individuals. Five years later, however, an amendment was passed allowing maimed persons to become members. See *(Journal of Proceedings,* 1870, p. 202; 1875, p. 1114).

Supreme Lodge sessions wanted the wording "white male" deleted. The convention referred the matter to appropriate committees. In 1966 the issue was again referred to committees, and in 1968 the matter failed to appear on the agenda of the convention.

Once an applicant for membership has been accepted by ball ballot, he, as in some orders previously discussed, is required to go through the required initiation rites. In preparation for the first rank (degree), the blindfolded candidate kneels before an open coffin containing a skeleton. He is asked a number of questions and finally given the "obligation" of secrecy and loyalty: "I solemnly promise that I will never reveal the password, grip, signs or any other secret or mystery of this rank, except in a lodge of this order . . . I will obey the laws . . . I will heed the teachings of this rank . . . So help me God—and may he keep me steadfast" (*Revised, Illustrated Ritual for Subordinate Lodges of Knights of Pythias,* 1945, pp. 21, 24, 25). For the second and third rank an oath or obligation is again required.

In public parades and processions some members of the society, similar to the Masonic Knights Templar and the Patriarchs in the Independent Order of Odd fellows, are clothed in the military costume of the Uniform Rank. This rank is under the control of the Supreme Lodge, and only members with the rank of Knight are eligible. "One of its purposes, beyond participating in the ceremonial of initiation which is said to be a masterpiece, is to supply a military branch" (Stevens, 1907, p. 165).

The Pythians, like some of the other Lodges, have their "fun" group, the Dramatic Order of the Knights of Khorassan (DOKK, referred to as "Doakes" by the members). This order was founded in 1894. The dress of this group in many ways resembles that of the Shriners. Only Knights of Pythias are eligible to join.

Officers in the Knights of Pythias are known as: Chancellor, Vice Chancellor, Prelate, Secretary, Treasurer, Master at Arms, Inner Guard, and Outer Guard. On the state and national level, the words "Grand" and "Supreme" are prefixed, respectively, to these positions.

Stevens in his *Cyclopedia of Fraternities* (1907) shows the

Knights of Pythias having about 450,000 members. Since then the order has declined markedly. Its 1967 roster listed 185,120 Knights. The trend in Nebraska and Vermont parallels the national decline. Nebraska, organized in 1869, had 1,243 knights in 1958, and by 1966 it had 970 (a 21.9 percent loss). The Vermont group, which dates from 1891, declined from 1,452 in 1936 to 1,005 members by 1945 (a 30.7 percent decrease).

PYTHIAN SISTERS

The history of the present-day Pythian Sisters is complicated by the fact that the present organization is the result of a consolidation which occurred in 1907. In 1888 the Supreme Lodge of the Knights of Pythias approved Joseph Addison Hill's ritual for a women's order. But the women preferred their own ritual written by Mrs. Alva A. Young (Stevens, 1907, p. 280). The latter ritual was accepted when the first Assembly of the Pythian Sisterhood was organized in Concord, New Hampshire, on February 22, 1888 (Jayne-Weaver and Wood, 1925, pp. 9-19). That same year the first temple of the Pythian Sisters of the World was formed in Warsaw, Indiana. Mr. Hill was again involved, and, in this instance, credited as founder of the order (Jayne-Weaver and Wood, 1925, pp. 9-19).

The Pythian Sisterhood (the Concord group) differed from the Pythian Sisters (the Warsaw group) in that it did not permit Knights of Pythias to become members, whereas the latter did. In 1894 the Pythian Sisters were in danger of losing their male (honorary) members since the Supreme Lodge of the Knights of Pythias did not permit any of its members to belong to an organization that used the name "Pythian" which was not under its control. This prompted the Pythian Sisters to change their name to Rathbone Sisters of the World (Stevens, 1907, pp. 280, 281).

In 1906 the Knights of Pythias permitted its members to belong to groups employing the name "Pythian." As a result of this action, the two women groups consolidated in 1907 and adopted the new name of Pythian Sisters (Jayne-Weaver and wood, 1925). This is the order in existence today.

The 1964 constitution of the subordinate (local) temples states:

> To be eligible to membership for initiation in a Temple [lodge], the person must be over sixteen years of age, of good character, and speak the English language, and be the wife, widow, sister, half-sister, sister-in-law, mother, stepmother or mother-in-law of a Knight of Pythias in good standing .... Persons having *Negro blood in their veins* [emphases not in the original] or unable to speak the English language are not eligible .... A Knight of Pythias must have taken the Rank of Page, Esquire and Knight before he is eligible to membership in a Temple .... *(Supreme Constitutions and Statutes, 1964, p. 88).*

By comparison, the Pythian Sisters have several things in common with the Order of the Eastern Star and the Rebekah Assembly: (1) neither group is accorded the status that is given to male lodges, even though each of these female orders was organized by a Mason, Odd Fellow, and Knight of Pythias, respectively; (2) neither group may initiate someone who is not related to a male lodge member (The Pythian Sisters' requirement in this respect is somewhat broader, but nevertheless limited); (3) all three have a ritual patterned to some extent after the male rituals; (4) all three support their respective male lodges.

Similar to other fraternal associations, the Pythian Sisters are characterized by a decreasing membership. The Grand Temple of Nebraska in 1925 boasted 1,595 Sisters. In 1958 the number had dwindled to 918 and to an even lower figure of 725 members (a loss of 21.0 percent) by 1967.

BENEVOLENT AND PROTECTIVE ORDER OF ELKS

Darrah, in his *History and Evolution of Freemasonry*, says: "The first Masonic Lodges held their meetings in a tavern where they had ready access to the tap room" (1967, p. 179). Drinking also played a role in the formation of the Elks. Whalen writes:

Had the New York state legislature not passed a law in 1866 closing the saloons on Sunday, the nation probably would not have seen the birth of the Benevolent and Protective Order of Elks. Many booze-loving citizens, including a group of actors in New York City, looked for ways to sidestep the new Sabbath Law. The actors rented a room first on Fourteenth Street and later on Bowery where they could refresh their spirits after a week behind the footlights (Whalen, 1966, p. 31).

These fun-loving actors soon organized and called themselves, the "Jolly Corks," derived from the "Cork Trick" which they skillfully performed on an unsuspecting newcomer who, as a victim, paid for the drinks and then could join the "in" group. Each Jolly Cork had a cork before him on the table. The newcomer was given one too. Before long the group would trick him into lifting his cork off the table. For this "error" he would have to buy the drinks. The victim apparently did not mind because he would joyfully wait to lend his hand in tricking someone new (Fehrenbach, 1967, pp. 5-7).

As the Jolly Corks' membership grew, new and more serious-minded men joined. It soon "became obvious there was both a need for and a chance to form a benevolent society for the theatrical world . . . " (Fehrenbach, 1967, p. 10). Thus in a regular session on Sunday, February 16, 1868, the Jolly Corks heard a committee report recommending that they be called "The Benevolent Protective Order of Elks" (BPOE). The symbol of the Elk was chosen because:

> The Elk attacked no other species and destroyed nothing—but it would fight valiantly in defense of its own life, and those of its females and young. The idea of an animal that lived in peace, but would fight to defend its rights to protect the weak and helpless, appealed strongly to the Corks (Fehrenbach, 1967, p. 13).

The Masonic influence in the early years of the Elks was obvious in that the new lodge used aprons as regalia, the term "tyler" for doorkeeper, the expression "Lodge of Sorrow" for deceased Elks, and the oath of secrecy. The official Elk publication by Fehrenbach, *Elkdom U.S.A.,* admits this: "Passwords, secret grips, blindfolds and aprons were borrowed from organizations ranging from Freemasons to Tammany Hall" (1967, p. 27). Today, however, the Elks have eliminated many of these customary lodge elements. "The apron went in 1895. The 'secret password' expired in 1899. The badge and grip died natural deaths in 1902 and 1904 respectively. The test oath and a few other extraneous things disappeared and the Elks began to be themselves and look less like a cross between the Masons and a college fraternity" (Fehrenbach, 1967, p. 43).

The current (1968-1969) membership requirement states: "No person shall be accepted as a member of the Order unless he be a white male citizen of the United States of America, of sound mind and body, of good character, not under the age of twenty-one years, and a believer in God" (*Constitution and Statues, BPOE*, 1968-1969, p. 70).

Only one degree is worked by the Elks lodge. The oath for this degree is lengthy and bears many similarities to the Masonic oaths, except that the Elks obligation does not invoke the penalties of death and physical mutilation. Elkdom has no so-called higher degrees or higher lodges.

With few exceptions, the organizational structure of the Elks is similar to other lodges. Its state organization is not known as the "Grand Lodge," but rather as "State Association." The term "Grand Lodge" in Elkdom refers to the national organization. Local meeting places are known as "Subordinate Lodges." Many committees have the same names and functions they do in other lodge groups.

In comparison with other fraternal societies, the Elks today differ remarkably in terms of membership growth. From 1959 to 1968, the grand lodge membership grew by 16.3 percent to a total of 1,452,187 Elks. The trend is also upward on the state level. The Kansas State Association, organized in 1907, currently (1969) has a membership of 30,174, an increase of over 15 percent since 1962.

SUMMARY AND CONCLUSION

In conclusion, two characteristics that are common to most of the orders discussed above deserve additional attention: the proud reference made to dignitaries that are, or were, members of fraternal organizations; the decline of membership.

The pride manifested by fraternal societies in referring to

prominent dignitaries as members of a fraternal group is not easily overlooked. The Masons boast of having had as members thirteen United States Presidents, from George Washington to Harry Truman.[14] In April, 1969, there were 45 United States Senators, 147 members in the House, four Supreme Court Justices, and 21 State Governors who were Masons (*Grand Lodge Bulletin,* Iowa, June, 1969, p. 173). The Knights of Pythias take pleasure in having had Franklin D. Roosevelt as their "brother." Similarly, Elkdom proudly claims John F. Kennedy, Harry S. Truman, Franklin D. Roosevelt, and that "one half of the United States Senate in the 1960's carried Elks cards" (Fehrenbach, 1967, p. 86).

Why most secret fraternal organizations have been declining for some fifteen to twenty years is an important question both for the lodges and for the scholar; however, there are different reasons why this question would be important to the two. Some lodge officials express the belief that television and fear of boarding buses in large urban centers keeps individuals from attending. Others believe apathy is largely responsible. It is unlikely that the first two reasons really contribute to the problem because in most lodges, the decline had begun prior to the advent of widespread television viewing. Fear of boarding buses fails to explain the membership decline that exists in non-urban areas; morever, most members probably attend their meetings by automobile. By "apathy," the leaders often mean that the lodge rituals frequently are no longer taken seriously. Even those who conduct (work) the ritual frequently read the ritual instead of committing it to memory. This, according to some lodge officials, destroys the beauty and meaning of the ritual and what the lodge stands for.

The fact that lodge rituals are not taken as seriously as they once were appears to indicate that most secret societies are caught in a cultural lag. Organizational change may be their only hope in averting continued membership decreases. The example of the Elks, who eliminated and modified many of their former practices, tends to lend credence to the organiza-

---

[14]For a listing of the United States Presidents who were Masons see Darrah (1967, pp. 380-381).

tional change argument, especially since the Elks' membership is growing quite rapidly.[15]

Whalen thinks the declining memberships are in part due to the lodges having failed to modify their "increasingly anachronistic racial bias," and that most college graduates today "see little value in such [lodge] membership" (Whalen, 1966, p. 66). On the other hand, racial discrimination has not adversely affected the Elks, who are as racially biased as any lodge group. Thus declining memberships may be more closely linked to outmoded rituals and oaths, that apparently are incongruous with our society's emphasis on "fun." Some authors (e.g., Klapp, 1969, pp. 182-186) suggest that fun is a new focal point of mass interest and that 'living it up' and engaging in the 'swinging life' are becoming major values. If this observation is valid, it helps explain why the Elks, who have placed increasing emphasis on providing "fun" for its members, are experiencing membership growth, while other lodge groups with austere, demanding rituals have been declining in recent years.

Another reason that merits consideration is that lodges have in recent years suffered a loss in status and influence. Warner, in his study of Jonesville, says: "the lodge is no longer a means of meeting the important men of the community, and membership is no longer a mark of esteem" (Warner, 1949, p. 120). That fraternal organizations once were important avenues to social status was noted by Max Weber as he visited the United States in 1904. In his discussion of "The Protestant Sects and the Spirit of Capitalism," he writes that lodge

> membership was acquired through balloting after investigation and determination of moral worth. And hence the badge in the buttonhole meant, 'I am a gentleman patented after investigation and probation and guaranteed by my membership.' Again, this meant, in business life above all, tested *credit worthiness*. One could observe that business opportunities were often decisively influenced by such legitimation (Weber, 1946, p. 308).

---

[15]Reference to changes made by the Elks was made earlier. One high-ranking grand lodge (national) Elk official thought their growth could largely be explained in the light of having eliminated, as he put it, the "tomfoolery" in initiation rites. Spoken in person to the author!

Weber continues: "These associations [lodges] were typical vehicles of social ascent into the circle of the entrepreneurial middle class. They served to diffuse and to maintain the bourgeois capitalist business ethos among the broad strata of the middle classes (the farmers included)" (1946, p. 308).

The observations by Warner and by Weber are underscored by comments that employees made to Dalton in one of the four firms he studied. One skilled workman said: "Promotion comes about by being a Mason . . . . Hell, all bosses are Masons." A foreman said to Dalton: "Nearly all the big boys are in the Yacht Club, and damn near all of 'em are Masons. You can't get a good job without being a Mason . . . ." Another employee remarked: "There's no promotion system whatever. Seniority, knowledge, or ability don't count . . . . I was once asked to join the Masons, and it was hinted that there'd be a good job in it for me" (Dalton, 1959, pp. 152, 154, 155).

Even if some allowance is made for over-emphasis, the statements made by the above employees probably give a fairly accurate representation of the status and influence that lodges once possessed.[16] Undoubtedly this helps explain the large memberships that fraternal societies had until one or two decades ago. The present membership decline in nearly all lodges may very well be due to a loss of status and influence. Another comment by Warner is appropriate here. He says: "even the Masons [who have always been the most influential and the most exclusive] are fast losing ground and being a high-degree Mason is no longer a sure step to social success" (Warner, 1949, p. 121).

All of the fraternal groups in the present study are seriously concerned about recent membership losses. Freemasons recently published reports and booklets specifically addressing themselves to the phenomenon of declining memberships (Masonic Service Association, 1960). Annual convention reports

---

[16]To join Masonry for personal gain is, of course, not formally sanctioned by Freemasonry. Mackey says an applicant desiring to become a Mason "must be *uninfluenced by mercenary motives* [sic]" (1967, p. 52). Departures from formal norms are, of course, common and widespread. Considerable sociological research has shown how informal norms frequently operate in spite of formal expectation. In this regard see Babchuk and Goode (1951), Roy (1952), and Blau (1955, pp. 427-442).

on membership and reports relative to the condition of the order frequently lament membership losses. However, none of the printed reports seem to recognize that dwindling lodge membership might in large measure be due to loss of status that most fraternal societies apparently have sustained in the past two decades or so. Hence, the efforts that many lodges are making in exhorting present members toward increases in membership and attendance will probably remain relatively unsuccessful, unless fraternal groups regain their former status, i.e., if it can be regained.

4

OLIGARCHY IN FRATERNAL ORGANIZATIONS

This chapter discusses the findings as they pertain to the hypotheses introduced earlier in Chapter 1. In most instances the results are discussed and evaluated in the light of previous research findings that dealt with similar or related issues.

ORGANIZATIONAL AGE AND OLIGARCHY

The first hypothesis examines the relationship between organizational age and oligarchic outcome in 16 statewide fraternal organizations by comparing leadership (executive officers and committee men) turnover data for two ten-year periods, the first ten years[1] and the most recent decade of each

---

[1]Relative to the first hypothesis, data for the first ten years were not available for one organization: the Pythian Sisters of Nebraska. This group had no published records available for the first three decades of its existence. Therefore, the figures for this organization reflect data from the fourth decade, 1930-1939. Two reasons prompted this substitution: one, it was felt that an organization thirty years old is still relatively young and would not be too drastically different from the other groups studied during their first ten years; two, even if the data for the 1930-1939 decade would reveal somewhat lower turnover rates due to the organization being in its fourth rather than its first decade, it would be permissible to include them because they would make it more difficult to accept Hypothesis 1.

organization. Two measures of leadership turnover are employed. One assesses the mean percentage of the total turnover of all officers and committee members for each ten-year span. (This is the principal measure.) The second measure focuses only on the percentage of officers and committee members who held office for five or more years during each ten-year period.

1. **Organizations are less oligarchic during the early or formative years of organizational life than during later periods.**

The principal measure of the dependent variable (which focuses on the turnover of *all* leaders, regardless of how many years they have been in office during a ten-year period) shows in Table 1 that the overall means for the first and most recent ten years were 69.4 and 39.4 percent, respectively. These results strongly support the hypothesis by showing that organizations have a substantially higher turnover of leaders during the early years of their existence than during the most recent decade. All organizations, except the Independent Order of Odd Fellows, had lower turnover rates during their most recent ten years.

Why the Odd Fellows differ from the other fraternal orders is not known at this point. Similar to the other groups, their membership grew during the first ten years, and declined during the most recent decade of their existence. Thus, the deviation does not appear to be due to membership variation. Second, their constitution did not impose limitations relative to tenure of office for the first ten years that differed from the order's most recent ten years.

The second measure of the dependent variable (percentage of leaders with five or more years of tenure in one or more positions during a ten year period) in Table 2 also supports the hypothesis. The data reveal that the mean percentage of leaders with five or more years of tenure for the first ten years is 21.3 and for the most recent decade is 31.4. Three organizations (the Royal Arch Masons, the Council, and the Odd Fellows, all from Nebraska) deviated from the predicted relationship by means of the second measure.

Even though the single deviation in Table 1 could not be explained, the three exceptions in Table 2 (including the Odd Fellows who deviated in both tables) might possibly be due to

TABLE 1*

MEAN PERCENTAGE OF LEADERSHIP TURNOVER
(EXECUTIVE OFFICERS AND COMMITTEE MEN)

Organization	First Ten Years		Most Recent Ten Years	
Masons - Nebr.	75	(1857-66)	24	(1958-67)
Masons - Conn.**	—	(1889-98)	28	(1958-67)
Royal Arch Masons - Nebr.	62	(1867-76)	51	(1959-68)
Royal Arch Masons - Conn.**	—	(1806-15)	24	(1955-64)
Knights Templar - Nebr.	65	(1871-80)	20	(1957-66)
Knights Templar - Conn.**	—	(1821-30)	22	(1959-68)
Grand Council - Nebr.	58	(1872-81)	48	(1955-64)
Grand Council - Conn.	67	(1873-82)	36	(1955-64)
Order of Eastern Star - Nebr.	74	(1875-84)	46	(1956-65)
Order of Eastern Star - Conn.	76	(1874-83)	44	(1958-67)
Ind. Order of Odd Fellows - Nebr.	68	(1858-67)	82	(1958-67)
Rebekahs - Nebr.	85	(1894-03)	48	(1955-64)
Knights of Pythias - Vermont	58	(1896-05)	20	(1936-45)
Knights of Pythias - Nebr.	70	(1869-78)	33	(1958-67)
Pythian Sisters - Nebr.	74	(1930-39)	70	(1959-68)
Elks - Kansas	71	(1907-16)	35	(1960-69)
Total	903		631	
Mean	69.4		39.4	

"t" = 5.80; df = 27; $p < .0005$

*Some of the details in the present table, namely, "Executive Officers and Committee Men" and the years that comprise the first and most recent decades of each organization, apply also to Tables 2 through 19, but are not repeated in their format.

**Data for these organizations were not complete for the first ten years. The listings of committee members and executive officers were irregularly recorded in their convention proceedings.

the nature of the second measure of leadership turnover, together with the relatively small memberships[2] that these groups had during the first ten years of their history. That is, the second index, by focusing only on leaders with five or more

---

[2]All three organizations had a mean membership of less than 500 members during the first ten years. Moreover, the first five years were especially characterized by small memberships which probably compelled leaders to stay in office for relatively longer periods in comparison to organizations with larger memberships.

TABLE 2
PERCENTAGE OF LEADERS WITH FIVE
OR MORE YEARS OF TENURE

Organization	First Ten Years	Most Recent Ten Years
Masons-Nebr.	33	38
Masons-Conn.	—	39
Royal Arch Masons-Nebr.	19	14
Royal Arch Masons-Conn.	—	44
Knights Templar-Nebr.	35	40
Knights Templar-Conn.	—	57
Grand Council-Nebr.	24	22
Grand Council-Conn.	20	50
Order of Eastern Star-Nebr.	20	20
Order of Eastern Star-Conn.	15	25
Ind. Order of Odd Fellows	48	11
Rebekahs-Nebr.	02	22
Knights of Pythias-Vermont	20	42
Knights of Pythias-Nebr.	22	30
Pythian Sisters-Nebr.	11	22
Elks-Kansas	09	27
Total	278	503
Mean	21.3	31.4

"t" = -2.197; df = 27; p < .025

years of tenure and ignoring those with less tenure, might reveal a more oligarchic leadership because a relatively small membership provides a rather limited number of potential leaders. This in turn probably compels a larger percentage of officeholders to govern for longer periods than would be true in organizations having large memberships.

Since executive officers usually are elected and committee members appointed, the data were also examined regarding possible differences in leadership turnover relative to these two types of leaders. Table 3 shows that the prediction in Hypothesis 1 holds for both types of leaders. Both groups became significantly more oligarchic over time.

Since Nebraska is an agricultural state and Connecticut an

TABLE 3

MEAN PERCENTAGE OF LEADERSHIP TURNOVER OF
EXECUTIVE OFFICERS AND COMMITTEE
MEN VIEWED SEPARATELY

Organization	Officers Only		Committee Members Only	
	First Ten Years	Most Recent Ten Years	*First Ten Years	Most Recent Ten Years
Masons-Nebr.	42	20	78	24
Masons-Conn.	21	22	–	28
Royal Arch Masons-Nebr.	39	15	65	55
Royal Arch Masons-Conn.	–	20	–	25
Knights Templar-Nebr.	29	14	70	22
Knights Templar-Conn.	–	16	–	23
Grand Council-Nebr.	28	22	63	54
Grand Council-Conn.	27	17	75	39
Order of Eastern Star-Nebr.	59	35	78	46
Order of Eastern Star-Conn.	–	44	81	43
Ind. Order of Odd Fellows-Nebr.	51	–	71	84
Rebekahs-Nebr.	11	20	94	50
Knights of Pythias-Vermont	–	–	61	19
Knights of Pythias-Nebr.	46	24	73	34
Pythian Sisters-Nebr.	–	–	78	75
Elks-Kansas	60	27	74	36
Total	413	296	961	657
Mean	37.5	22.7	73.9	41.0

Officers only; "t" = 3.05; df = 22; p < .005 Committee members only; "t" =
5.93; df = 27; p < .0005

industrial state,[3] it might be argued that the data in Tables 1, 2,
and 3 should be controlled for in terms of such a distinction.
Themes such as the "Organization Man," "Organizational
Society," and "Bureaucratic Values" (Whyte, 1957; Presthus,
1962; Miller and Swanson, 1958) that are frequently depicted
as concomitants of an industrial environment, suggest that
organizations in an industrial state (Connecticut) may be more

[3]This distinction is supported by *Comptons Pictured Encyclopedia* (1966 ed.)
See volumes X, 107-122 and III, 519-535 respectively.

bureaucratic or oligarchic than in an agricultural region (Nebraska and Kansas). Such thinking gains further support in the light of the Populist Movement (an ideology which opposed industrial values)[4] that was particularly widespread and important in the 1890's in Nebraska, Kansas, and other Mid-Western States, but relatively unimportant in the industrial East (Connecticut and other contiguous states).

The data, however, reveal that an industrial area or agricultural region apparently has very little affect on oligarchic or non-oligarchic outcome of fraternal groups. In both the agricultural environment (Table 4) and the industrial environment (Table 5), the leadership turnover is significantly lower during the most recent ten years than it was during the first decade of the organizations' existence. The first and most recent ten years for the Nebraska-Kansas groups, reflect mean percentages of 70.2 and 45.7, respectively; for the Connecticut associations the mean percentages are 71.5 and 30.8, respectively.[5]

The second measure of leadership turnover indicates a slightly different pattern (Table 6). The Nebraska-Kansas associations, with a mean of 24.6 percent of its leaders holding office for five or more years during the last ten years, as opposed to a mean of 22.2 percent for the first decade, do not show a significant difference. The Connecticut organizations, however, with a mean of 43.0 percent for the most recent ten years, and a mean of 17.5 percent for the first ten-year period, do show a significant difference.

A casual comparison of the first measure (Tables 4 and 5) with the second measure (Tables 6 and 7) appears to suggest that the findings are inconsistent. However, a closer examination shows that the results are quite compatible. First, the means which are virtually the same for the first ten years in

---

4One noted scholar describes Populism as a movement that sought to "save agricultural America from the devouring jaws of industrial America" (Hicks, 1931, p. 237). See also Pollack (1962).

5Since Table 5 does not list means of the mean percentage (the Mann-Whitney U test does not require these data), they are cited for the convenience of the reader. The Mann-Whitney U test was primarily employed in Table 5 and several other tables because of unequal and small sample size. See Bonneau (1960).

TABLE 4

MEAN PERCENTAGE OF LEADERSHIP TURNOVER
NEBRASKA-KANSAS ORGANIZATIONS

Organization	First Ten Years	Most Recent Ten Years
Masons	75	24
Royal Arch Masons	62	51
Knights Templar	65	20
Grand Council	58	48
Order of Eastern Star	74	46
Ind. Order of Odd Fellows	68	82
Rebekahs	85	48
Knights of Pythias	70	33
Pythian Sisters	74	70
Elks	71	35
Total	702	457
Mean	70.2	45.7

"t" = 3.93; df = 18; p<.0005

TABLE 5

MEAN PERCENTAGE OF LEADERSHIP TURNOVER
CONNECTICUT ORGANIZATIONS

Organization	First Ten Years	Most Recent Ten Years
Masons	–	28
Royal Arch Masons	–	24
Knights Templar	–	22
Grand Council	67	36
Order of Eastern Star	76	44

$U = O$; $N_1 = 2$; $N_2 = 5$; $p = .047$

Tables 4 and 5 are also relatively similar for the first decade in Tables 6 and 7. Second, the data in Tables 5 and 7 are highly congruous in terms of statistical significance. The notable

TABLE 6

PERCENTAGE OF LEADERS WITH FIVE
OR MORE YEARS OF TENURE
NEBRASKA-KANSAS ORGANIZATIONS

Organization	First Ten Years	Most Recent Ten Years
Masons	33	38
Royal Arch Masons	19	14
Knights Templar	35	40
Grand Council	24	22
Order of Eastern Star	20	20
Ind. Order of Odd Fellows	48	11
Rebekahs	02	22
Knights of Pythias	22	30
Pythian Sisters	11	22
Elks	09	27
Total	223	246
Mean	22.3	24.6

"t" = -.463; df = 18; N.S.

TABLE 7

PERCENTAGE OF LEADERS WITH FIVE
OR MORE YEARS OF TENURE
CONNECTICUT ORGANIZATIONS

Organization	First Ten Years	Most Recent Ten Years
Masons	—	39
Royal Arch Masons	—	44
Knights Templar	—	57
Grand Council	20	50
Order of Eastern Star	15	25

$U = O$; $N_1 = 2$; $N_2 = 5$; $p = .047$

difference is between Tables 4 and 6.

This difference is not due to size, since the mean size for the Nebraska-Kansas societies is 17,516 and for the Connecticut groups is 17,213 members. Instead it appears that the difference is largely a function of organizational age (the mean age for the Nebraska-Kansas associations in 89.9 years and 134.0 years for the Connecticut orders) and partially due to the nature of the second measure, which assesses leadership turnover by focusing only on individuals who have been in office for five or more years and ignores those with less tenure. In comparison to the first (principal) measure (which focuses on all leaders, regardless of how long they have held office during a ten-year span), the second index, being more restrictive in nature, appears to yield slightly different results, together with the variable of organizational age, i.e., *if the organizations in both geographic areas were the same age, they would probably reveal similar turnover rates by means of the second measure.*

Further discussion regarding organizational age and oligarchy will be postponed until the findings for Hypotheses 2 and 4 are considered. The independent variables (organizational size and spatial distribution of members, respectively) of these two hypotheses will be utilized for control purposes relative to Hypothesis 1. Until that analysis, the results pertaining to the first hypothesis may be summarized as follows: oligarchic leadership appears to be the function of organizational age in that fraternal organizations have significantly higher rates of leadership turnover during their first ten years of existence than they have during their most recent decade. This trend does not vary with geographic environment.

ORGANIZATIONAL SIZE AND OLIGARCHY

The data pertaining to the next hypothesis not only permit an examination of the relationship between organizational size and leadership outcome, but also permit controlling for age of organization as the effects of organizational size are examined.

2. **Large-scale organizations are more oligarchic than small ones.**

Since organizational age and size are somewhat directly related (r = .238, df = 14) in the present study, the question arises whether the trend toward oligarchic leadership perhaps is not a function of organizational size rather than age. Most discussions, theoretical or empirical, concerned with oligarchy frequently underscore the importance of organizational size and virtually ignore organizational age.[6] Indeed, even Michels (1959) gives little attention to age of organization,[7] but sees size of organization as a significant factor in accounting for his iron law of oligarchy. (Organizational age will be discussed at greater length later in this chapter.)

In Chapter 1 it was noted that Cassinelli adopts Michels' suggestion that organizations with about 10,000 members are likely to be oligarchic. If this figure is employed, the data in Tables 8 and 9 provide one test of the second hypothesis. Table 8 depicts large secret societies and Table 9 reflects small fraternal orders. The largest of the small groups in this study has a membership of 8,274, and the smallest of the large groups has 10,181 members. The large organizations ranged from 10,181 to 46,506 members, the small ones from 819 to 8,274.

The difference between the overall means for the large organizations for the first ten years and for the latter ten years (Table 8) is significant at the .001 level. For the small organizations the differences between the overall means for the two decades is significant at the .005 level. This indicates that organizational size does not seem to be related to oligarchic outcome. If the small difference in the level of significance between the large organizations in Table 8 (p < .001) and the small lodge groups in Table 9 (p<.005) is to be considered at all, it must be noted that the large secret orders in this instance are also older. The second and more restrictive measure of oligarchic outcome shows that large organizations in Table 10 (mean percentage for the first ten years and most recent decade are 15.8 and 30.7, respectively) are more oligarchic than are the

---

[6]Two recent studies which have taken organizational age into consideration are those of Raphael (1965) and Marcus (1966).

[7]Organizational size has been treated as a critical variable in sociological literature ever since Durkheim (1952). See also Haire (1959), Caplow (1957), Grusky (1961), Presthus (1962), Weber (1947), Michels (1959).

TABLE 8

MEAN PERCENTAGE OF LEADERSHIP TURNOVER
IN LARGE ORGANIZATIONS

Organization	First Ten Years	Most Recent Ten Years
Masons-Nebr.	75	24
Masons-Conn.	–	28
Royal Arch Masons-Conn.	–	24
Order of Eastern Star-Conn.	76	44
Order of Eastern Star-Nebr.	74	46
Rebekahs-Nebr.	85	48
Elks-Kansas	71	35

$U = O; N_1 = 5; N_2 = 7; p = .001$

TABLE 9

MEAN PERCENTAGE OF LEADERSHIP TURNOVER
IN SMALL ORGANIZATIONS

Organization	First Ten Years	Most Recent Ten Years
Royal Arch Masons-Nebr.	62	51
Knights Templar-Nebr.	65	20
Knights Templar-Conn.	–	22
Grand Council-Nebr.	58	48
Grand Council-Conn.	67	36
Ind. Order of Odd Fellows-Nebr.	68	82
Knights of Pythias-Vermont	58	20
Knights of Pythias-Nebr.	70	33
Pythian Sisters-Nebr.	74	70
Total	522	382
Mean	65.2	42.4

"t" = 2.97; df = 15; p < .005

small associations in Table 11 (mean percentages for the first ten years and last ten years are 24.8 and 32.0). However, as we mentioned above in connection with Tables 4 and 6, the second measure alone, which focuses only on a given segment of leaders (those with five or more years of tenure), cannot be seen as confirming the hypothesis regarding size and political outcome. Moreover, the smaller lodge groups in Table 11 have not been in existence as long as the larger ones in Table 10.

TABLE 10

PERCENTAGE OF LEADERS WITH FIVE
OR MORE YEARS OF TENURE
IN LARGE ORGANIZATIONS

Organization	First Ten Years	Most Recent Ten Years
Masons-Nebr.	33	38
Masons-Conn.	–	39
Royal Arch Masons-Conn.	–	44
Order of Eastern Star-Conn.	15	25
Order of Eastern Star-Nebr.	20	20
Rebekahs-Nebr.	02	22
Elks-Kansas	09	27

$U = 4.5$; $N_1 = 5$; $N_2 = 7$; $p = .024$

TABLE 11

PERCENTAGE OF LEADERS WITH FIVE
OR MORE YEARS OF TENURE
IN SMALL ORGANIZATIONS

Organization	First Ten Years	Most Recent Ten Years
Royal Arch Masons-Nebr.	19	14
Knights Templar-Nebr.	35	40
Knights Templar-Conn.	–	57
Grand Council-Nebr.	24	22
Grand Council-Conn.	20	50
Ind. Order of Odd Fellows-Nebr.	48	11
Knights of Pythias-Vermont	20	42
Knights of Pythias-Nebr.	22	30
Pythian Sisters-Nebr.	11	22
Total	199	288
Mean	24.8	32.0

"t" = -1.10; df = 15; N.S.

In attempting to ascertain whether oligarchic outcome is really independent of organizational size, an alternate test was utilized. A difference of means test ("t" test) was employed to see whether the mean leadership turnover rate of the large organizations differed from that of the small fraternal orders during their most recent ten years. The result was not significant statistically ("t" = .796; df=14).

The apparent lack of association between size of organization and leadership turnover concurs with what Raphael found in her sample of local unions in Cook County, Illinois. "In the total sample of organizations, the form of political organization does not vary with size of membership" (Raphael, 1965, p. 280).

On the other hand, other reports indicate that organizational size apparently is related to oligarchy. Seidman (1953) concluded that middle-sized one-plant local unions (not more than a few hundred members) displayed the most democratic form of leadership structure. Lipset, Trow, and Coleman observed that larger locals manifested a greater interest in national union politics and that political opposition also was greater with respect to policies of the incumbents (1956, pp. 410-439). Faunce (1962) reported that large local unions contributed more to the democratic processes on the national level. For example, members of large locals were more likely to attend convention caucuses and saw referendums as more important on significant issues than did members in small locals.

At first glance, it may appear that the findings by Seidman, Faunce, and Lipset are inconsistent with the findings reported with respect to Hypothesis 1, since the data for this hypothesis show that oligarchic outcome is not related to size of organization. However, closer examination of the above studies shows that the inconsistencies are more apparent than real because these inquiries employed different operational definitions of organizational democracy.

Frequently when size of organization (large or small) is seen affecting the democratic process of a given organization, reference is made to different dimensions of democracy. Some of these include: attendance at regular meetings, leadership turnover, opposition to incumbents, referendums, policy-making participation, or attendance at conventions.

Hence, merely to say that democracy in organizations is dependent on size is inadequate, unless it is specified which particular aspects of democracy are under examination. An appropriate illustration is Faunce's study of the United Automobile Workers. He found that small local unions were more democratic internally than large locals, i.e., small unions had a greater proportion of their members attend local meetings; they also had a greater turnover of leadership. However, in analyzing large local unions, relative to contributing to democratic processes on the national union level, Faunce found that small locals reflected a low democratic profile, given indexes other than rates of membership participation and leadership turnover in local unions. For instance, delegates from small locals were less active in national convention politics, objected less to the idea of union officers expecting them to vote a certain way, and saw less value in referendums. Thus, before studies can be compared purporting to show either a direct or inverse relationship between organizational size and democracy, it must be ascertained whether similar components of democratic behavior are evaluated. Failure to do so only obscures the problem.

Given this discussion, the present findings pertaining to Hypothesis 2 probably are most appropriately compared to other investigations that have focused on the dimension of leadership turnover. In this regard two studies are particularly relevant; one by Faunce (1962) and one by Brown (1956). Both essentially reveal the same results. Faunce found small local unions had more frequent turnover of officials than did large locals. Similarly, Brown reports that there was a significant inverse relationship between union size and leadership turnover.

The results of these two reports which differ from the findings in the present inquiry can be accounted for quite readily. First, neither Brown nor Faunce controlled for organizational age in assessing the effects of organizational size. Had they controlled for age of organization their findings might have been different. Second, Brown's findings are based on only one organization; data from a number of organizations might have yielded different results. Third, since Faunce's study reflects information at the local union level, and the present study on the state level, the question arises to what extent one should expect similar results when studies focus on different levels of aggregation.[8]

In summary, the present study shows that the relationship between organizational age and oligarchic leadership continues to hold even after controlling for size of organization. The data indicate that size of organization is at best only indirectly related to oligarchic rule in fraternal orders.

ORGANIZATIONAL COMPLEXITY AND OLIGARCHY

The third hypothesis, which focuses on the relationship between organizational complexity and oligarchic outcome, has never been examined empirically (as far as the author knows) prior to the present investigation. No explicit discussions are available in the literature regarding organizational complexity and Michels' iron law of oligarchy. For the most part, those studies that refer to the problem consist only of implications, rather than direct statements or cmpirical findings. Therefore, the next hypothesis must be viewed as being primarily exploratory in nature.

3. **Complex organizations become more oligarchic over time than do organizations that are less-complex.**

In order to designate the fraternal groups in the present sample as "complex" and "less-complex," the data (convention resolutions and reports) were dichotomized at the mean; organizations which had a mean score of 35 or more resolutions and reports were considered "complex," those below 35 as "less-complex."

While the data in Tables 12 and 13 indicate that both the complex and less-complex groups are more oligarchic during their most recent ten years, they also reveal that the complex groups in Table 12 do *not* become more oligarchic over time

---

[8]For further discussion relative to the problem of making inferences from different levels of aggregation see the article by Davis, Spaeth, and Huson (1961). Other related discussions may be found in Lazarsfeld and Menzel (1961) and Scott (1964).

than do the less-complex groups in Table 13. In fact, the less-complex organizations became more oligarchic than the complex groups. The second measure of leadership turnover reveals results very similar in Tables 14 and 15.

TABLE 12

MEAN PERCENTAGE OF LEADERSHIP TURNOVER
IN COMPLEX ORGANIZATIONS

Organization	First Ten Years	Most Recent Ten Years
Masons-Nebr.	75	24
Masons-Conn.	–	28
Royal Arch Masons-Nebr.	62	51
Order of Eastern Star-Conn.	76	44
Ind. Order of Odd Fellows-Nebr.	68	82
Rebekahs-Nebr.	85	48

$U = 4; N_1 = 5; N_2 = 6; p = .026$

TABLE 13

MEAN PERCENTAGE OF LEADERSHIP TURNOVER
IN LESS COMPLEX ORGANIZATIONS

Organization	First Ten Years	Most Recent Ten Years
Royal Arch Masons-Conn.	–	24
Knights Templar-Nebr.	65	20
Knights Templar-Conn.	–	22
Order of Eastern Star-Nebr.	74	46
Knights of Pythias-Vermont	58	20
Knights of Pythias-Nebr.	70	33

$U = O; N_1 = 4; N_2 = 6; p = .005$

In attempting to explain why fraternal orders of lesser complexity tend to be more oligarchic, the study of Lipset, Trow, and Coleman, *Union Democracy,* is helpful.Their study reports that political cleavage and conflict fostered democracy

TABLE 14

PERCENTAGE OF LEADERS WITH FIVE
OR MORE YEARS OF TENURE IN
COMPLEX ORGANIZATIONS

Organization	First Ten Years	Most Recent Ten Years
Masons-Nebr.	33	38
Masons-Conn.	–	39
Royal Arch Masons-Nebr.	19	14
Order of Eastern Star-Conn.	15	25
Ind. Order of Odd Fellows-Nebr.	48	11
Rebekahs-Nebr.	02	22

$U = 14; N_1 = 5; N_2 = 6;$ N.S.

TABLE 15

PERCENTAGE OF LEADERS WITH FIVE
OR MORE YEARS OF TENURE IN
LESS COMPLEX ORGANIZATIONS

Organization	First Ten Years	Most Recent Ten Years
Royal Arch Masons-Conn.	–	44
Knights Templar-Nebr.	35	40
Knights Templar-Conn.	–	57
Order of Eastern Star-Nebr.	20	20
Knights of Pythias-Vermont	20	42
Knights of Pythias-Nebr.	22	30

$U = 4; N_1 = 4; N_2 = 6; p = .057$

in the International Typographical Union. Given this explanation, together with the present investigation's operational definition of complexity (number of convention reports and resolutions), it is possible that less-complex organizations probably elicit or arouse less interest, tension, and concern than do complex fraternal orders. Hence, less-complex groups tend to become more oligarchic over time.

Finally, it is interesting to note that if these results are viewed from the perspective of organizational size, the data show that less-complex groups are considerably smaller (mean = 10,938) than the complex fraternal orders (mean = 24,502). Thus, the greater trend toward oligarchy in Tables 13 and 15 does not appear to be a function of large size.

In short, the findings pertaining to the relationship between organizational complexity and oligarchy show that complex fraternal groups become less oligarchic over time than do the less-complex ones. This finding is contrary to what was predicted.

SPATIAL DISTRIBUTION OF MEMBERSHIPS
AND OLIGARCHY

The next hypothesis tested is an outgrowth of the social-interaction model. This model assumes that an organization's spatial distribution of members affects informal communication and interaction, which are seen as important prerequisites for organizational democracy.

4. **Organizations with spatially dispersed memberships become more oligarchic over time than do spatially concentrated organizations.**

Spatial distribution of members is viewed in the light of the number of chapters per fraternal society. The organizations in the sample were assigned to one of two classes: Those having spatially *concentrated* members (12 to 46 chapters), and those having spatially *dispersed* members (104 to 272 chapters). There were no organizations with members distributed between 47 and 103 chapters. It might be argued that this two-fold division of organizations (those with spatially concentrated and spatially dispersed members), separated empirically, not arbitrarily, by a pronounced gap in the number of local chapters, provides data that carry considerable import relative to the fourth hypothesis, regardless of the outcome.

The data in Table 16 (spatially dispersed members) and in Table 17 (spatially concentrated members) show that fraternal

TABLE 16

MEAN PERCENTAGE OF LEADERSHIP TURNOVER
IN ORGANIZATIONS WITH SPATIALLY
DISPERSED MEMBERS

Organization	First Ten Years	Most Recent Ten Years
Masons-Nebr.	75	24
Masons-Conn.	–	28
Order of Eastern Star-Conn.	76	44
Order of Eastern Star-Nebr.	74	46
Ind. Order of Odd Fellows-Nebr.	68	82
Rebekahs-Nebr.	85	48

$U = 4; N_1$ 5; $N_2 = 6; p = .026$

TABLE 17

MEAN PERCENTAGE OF LEADERSHIP TURNOVER
IN ORGANIZATIONS WITH SPATIALLY
CONCENTRATED MEMBERS

Organization	First Ten Years	Most Recent Ten Years
Royal Arch Masons-Conn.	–	24
Royal Arch Masons-Nebr.	62	51
Knights Templar-Nebr.	65	20
Knights Templar-Conn.	–	22
Grand Council-Nebr.	58	48
Grand Council-Conn.	67	36
Knights of Pythias-Vermont	58	20
Knights of Pythias-Nebr.	70	33
Pythian Sisters-Nebr.	74	70
Elks-Kansas	71	35
Total	525	359
Mean	65.6	35.9

"t" = 5.15; df = 16; p < .0005

orders with spatially dispersed members became less oligarchic over time than did organizations with spatially concentrated members. The second measure of leadership turnover in Tables 18 and 19 essentially reflects the same tendency.

TABLE 18

PERCENTAGE OF LEADERS WITH FIVE OR MORE
YEARS OF TENURE IN ORGANIZATIONS WITH
SPATIALLY DISPERSED MEMBERS

Organization	First Ten Years	Most Recent Ten Years
Masons-Nebr.	33	38
Masons-Conn.	—	39
Order of Eastern Star-Conn.	15	25
Order of Eastern Star-Nebr.	20	20
Ind. Order of Odd Fellows-Nebr.	48	11
Rebekahs-Nebr.	02	22

$U = 12.5$; $N_1 = 5$; $N_2 = 6$; N.S.

TABLE 19

PERCENTAGE OF LEADERS WITH FIVE OR MORE
YEARS OF TENURE IN ORGANIZATIONS WITH
SPATIALLY CONCENTRATED MEMBERS

Organization	First Ten Years	Most Recent Ten Years
Royal Arch Masons-Conn.	—	44
Royal Arch Masons-Nebr.	19	14
Knights Templar-Nebr.	35	40
Knights Templar-Conn.	—	57
Grand Council-Nebr.	24	22
Grand Council-Conn.	20	50
Knights of Pythias-Vermont	20	42
Knights of Pythias-Nebr.	22	30
Pythian Sisters-Nebr.	11	22
Elks-Kansas	09	27
Total	160	348
Mean	20.0	34.8

"t" = -2.82; df = 16; p < .01

This finding, which shows organizations with spatially dispersed members to be less oligarchic over time than organizations with spatially concentrated members, is not only contrary to the expectation of the fourth hypothesis, but it also fails to support Raphael's findings. She found organizations with widely dispersed members to be more oligarchic than those with spatially concentrated members. The present inquiry reveals the opposite.

Raphael proposed that spatial concentration of members facilitates informal communication and interaction which give rise to a democratic form of organization, while organizations with spatially dispersed members provide less of an opportunity for informal communication and interaction and, as a result, become more oligarchic in form (Raphael, 1965).

The social-interaction model, however, failed to explain the findings in the present investigation. This discrepancy is readily explained. Operationally, it should be recalled that the organizations with spatially dispersed members are those with the largest number of chapters. A large number of chapters also means a large number of local leaders who probably contend for offices in the state organization. Such behavior could very well account for higher rates of leadership turnover, while groups with spatially concentrated members would have fewer local leaders seeking positions on the state level, and hence a greater tendency toward an oligarchic leadership. This explanation appears highly tenable especially for organizations on a statewide level.

A second noteworthy item relative to the spatial distribution of members pertains to another finding in Raphael's study. She found that when spatial distribution of members was held constant the relationship between age of organization and oligarchy disappeared. "The common occurrence of 'oligarchic' political organization in the old local unions is perhaps better attributed to their spatially dispersed memberships, and perhaps only indirectly to bureaucratization through age of the organization" (1965, p. 278). This conclusion is not supported by the data in the present investigation. Not only are the organizations with spatially dispersed memberships in the present study less oligarchic than those with spatially concentrated memberships, but both types of organizations (those with spatially dispersed and spatially concentrated members) become more oligarchic over time (Tables 16 and 17). Thus, Hypothesis 1 is strongly supported, namely, that fraternal organizations are less oligarchic during the early, formative years of their existence than during their later periods, even after controlling for spatial distribution of members.

The present findings, which contradict Raphael's results, are probably best explained in the light of the research techniques employed and in terms of the time dimension. In the present research a longitudinal method of analysis was employed. This permitted comparisons for two periods of time: the first ten years and the most recent ten years of each organization in the present study. This approach apparently tapped data that the alternate method of studying organizations cross-sectionally (Raphael's method) did not. Had the longitudinal approach been used in Raphael's research, it is conceivable that the findings for both studies might have been more compatible.

The fact that the findings relative to Hypotheses 2 and 4 show oligarchic outcome to be essentially unaffected by organizational size and spatial distribution of members appears to indicate that organizational age is a crucial variable in organizations becoming oligarchic. Several plausible explanations which account for the salience of organizational age can be cited. Particularly plausible are the notions of membership apathy, vested interests on the part of leaders, hero worship, and fear of leadership change.

A rather common explanation cited in accounting for an oligarchic leadership is membership apathy.[9] The present data pertaining to the relationship between organizational age and oligarchy may appropriately be interpreted in the context of rank and file apathy. However, in focusing upon the condition of apathy it will be viewed from the perspective of time (organizational age), i.e., in terms of a developmental process that occurs over time.

---

[9]The literature abounds with reference to apathy. Dumas referred to apathy as "our fifth column." See John M. Dumas (1947). Another writer asks: "What is this apathy that infects John Smith, American citizen, to the point where in utter frustration, despair, and hopelessness he exchanges life for existence?" (Alinsky, 1946, p. 66). Other publications referring to apathy are Riesman and Glazer (1965), Dean (1960), and Barber (1965).

An examination of the history of social movements lends credence to the idea that apathy requires time to develop because the initial, formative periods of organizational life are frequently characterized by intense loyalty and enthusiastic participation. Describing the incipient phase of social movements, one author writes: "Loyalty is usually intense and group cohesion strong, re-enforced by personal contacts between founder and disciples and by the emotional momentum generated through participation in a new undertaking" (C. Wendell King, 1956, p. 43). Loyalty and interest, however, subside over time. Some of the literature on voluntary associations suggests that the process of formalization retards loyal and enthusiastic involvement which characterizes early organizational life (Tsouderos, 1955; Chapin and Tsouderos, 1955). In addition, lofty ideals and goals, which many of the organizing and more or less initial members bring to the organization, become tempered and subdued in time, either through fulfillment or apparent fulfillment. After this apathy follows.[10]

Generalizing from the above discussion to the organizations in the present sample regarding organizational age and oligarchic outcome, it might be concluded that fraternal associations, like many other collectivities, in their early history have rather highly enthusiastic and active participants, but in time interest wanes, giving way to apathy which in turn encourages an oligarchic leadership.

A second reason that may help explain why fraternal societies are more oligarchic during later stages of their life cycle is the matter of possible vested interests on the part of leaders. Once a leader has held office for some time a certain amount of prestige, status, and other rewards accrue to him. Relinquishing one's office or position probably means loss of status and perhaps esteem. Thus an effort is made to retain one's leadership role in the organizational structure. Michels cites this factor as a problem with reference to trade-union leaders (1959, pp. 297-315, 373).

---

[10]That fulfillment or apparent fulfillment of goals greatly reduces an organization's vitality is clearly shown in Krueger's (1968) discussion of the Keep Our Doctors Committee in Saskatchewan.

A third reason, perhaps, that might be interwoven with apathy and vested interests is the phenomenon of "hero worship" (Hook, 1943, pp. 229-245). Once leaders have served for a relatively long period there develops among the rank and file a "fondness for the faces they know" (Duverger, 1954, p. 160), or a "cult for the leaders, who are regarded as heroes" (Michels, 1959, p. 53). Klapp (1964; 1969) believes that hero worship gives people vicarious and shared experiences. Given this assumption, it is possible that hero worship (probably also present to some extent in fraternal organizations) contributes to membership apathy by permitting the rank and file to think they have met their organizational responsibilities through the vicarious experiences derived from being enamored with their organization's leaders, although in reality they are inactive and uninvolved. Hero worship might also be viewed as contributing to the leaders' vested interests. The status and esteem (already discussed above) that leaders enjoy may be reinforced by hero worship in that leaders, who receive considerable attention and honor, may conclude that the members want them to remain in office, and so they exert effort to that end.

A fourth factor may be the fear of leadership change. Studies in social change reveal that people frequently resist change because they dread the new and unfamiliar. A similar process may be operative relative to change in leadership personnel. From past performances, the rank and file undoubtedly derive considerable comfort in knowing what to expect from a stable, familiar leadership. *In time* this preference develops a tradition that strongly encourages retention of previous, familiar leaders.

ORGANIZATIONAL SIZE, AGE, COMPLEXITY
AND OLIGARCHY

Finally, the present research examines whether spatial distribution of members in organizations is related to organizational size, age, or complexity.

5. Organizations with spatially dispersed memberships differ
from those with spatially concentrated memberships in that
they are: (a) larger; (b) older; (c) more complex.

The data pertaining to Hypothesis 5a (Table 20) show that
organizations with widely dispersed memberships are indeed
larger than associations which have less widely dispersed
memberships. These results (analyzed by means of Fisher Exact
Probability Test) not only support the hypothesis, but also
concur with Raphael's (1965) data.

TABLE 20

ORGANIZATIONAL MEMBERSHIP SIZE

	9,999 Or Less	10,000 Or More	Total
Dispersed memberships	1	5	6
Concentrated memberships	8	2	10
Total	9	7	16

p = .023

In order to categorize associations into two age groups the
mean (101 years) of all sixteen fraternal societies in the sample
was utilized. The data in Table 21 show that Hypothesis 5b,
which predicts that organizations with spatially dispersed
memberships are older, is not supported. Unlike Raphael's data
which showed a significant relationship between spatially
dispersed memberships and organizational age, the results in the
present study provide additional support for Hypothesis 1,
namely, that age is directly related to an oligarchic leadership
structure.

TABLE 21

AGE OF ORGANIZATION

	100 Years Or Less	101 Years Or More	Total
Dispersed memberships	3	3	6
Concentrated memberships	7	3	10
Total	10	6	16

p = .390; N.S.

The final prediction in the current study, Hypothesis 5c, employed the previous measure of complexity (number of convention resolutions and reports). The results (Table 22) indicate that organizations having spatially dispersed members are significantly more complex than their counterparts. This latter finding is consistent with the results of Hypothesis 3 where complex organizations were found to be less oligarchic than the less complex associations. It is also consistent with the data in Hypothesis 4, where organizations with spatially dispersed members were less oligarchic than those with spatially concentrated members.

TABLE 22

ORGANIZATIONAL COMPLEXITY*

	34 Or Less Reports And Resolutions	35 Or More Reports And Resolutions	Total
Dispersed memberships	1	5	6
Concentrated memberships	5	1	6
Total	6	6	12

p = .039
*Four organizations are omitted due to lack of complete data relative to complexity information.

In summary, the results of Hypothesis 5a reveal that fraternal organizations with widely dispersed members are larger than are those with less widely dispersed members. The data in Hypothesis 5b indicate that there is no relationship between spatial distribution of members and organizational age, while the figures in Hypothesis 5c depict organizations with spatially dispersed members to be more complex than their counterparts with spatially concentrated members.

5

SUMMARY
AND
CONCLUSIONS

The primary objective of the present study was to examine Michels' iron law of oligarchy in the context of expressive voluntary associations, specifically fraternal societies. To achieve this end a longitudinal design, which collected data from each organization's first ten and most recent ten years, was employed.

The data gathered by means of this longitudinal technique served several useful purposes: 1) They provided a measure of organizational age that departed from merely counting the number of years a given organization had been in existence prior to the time of being studied. In short, age of organization was measured without resorting to arbitrary cut-off dates in order to classify an organization either as "young" or "old." 2) They permitted comparing the effect of organizational age upon the dependent variable (oligarchic outcome) over two different ten-year periods. 3) They enabled viewing organizational size, complexity, and spatial distribution of members in a manner substantially different from previous cross-sectional studies. 4) Comparatively speaking, they revealed a more rectilinear perspective of organizational change relative to the process of leadership turnover.

Sixteen statewide fraternal organizations were selected. Ten organizations were chosen from two neighboring agricultural states (Nebraska and Kansas), and five groups were selected from an industrial state (Connecticut). These two regions were chosen on the assumption that they represented two different political environments; the industrial area, given to bureaucratic values (it was reasoned) might have organizations that are relatively oligarchic; the agricultural region, once characterized by agrarian radicalism might have organizations that are relatively less oligarchic. Thus, the two different regions were selected to ascertain whether oligarchic outcome in fraternal organizations varied with regional environment. In addition to the Connecticut and Nebraska-Kansas groups, the study included one fraternal order from Vermont. However, this latter group was not included in the industrial-versus-agricultural analysis.

The fact that the present study relative to Hypothesis 1 found fraternal organizations significantly more oligarchic during their most recent ten years than during their first decade of existence, apparently indicates that the present longitudinal measure tapped effects of organizational age that previous measures failed to tap. For instance, Raphael's (1965) cross-sectional study of local unions found oligarchic outcome to be independent of organizational age.

The effect of organizational age continued to hold also after two other variables, size of organization, and spatial distribution of memberships, were controlled. That is, neither organizational size nor spatial distribution appeared to influence the pattern of leadership turnover in fraternal organizations. Both the large and small associations showed essentially similar oligarchic trends over time, and there was no significant difference between the organizations with spatially dispersed and spatially concentrated memberships relative to age of organization.

The absence of any relationship between organizational size and political outcome in the present study concurred with one other study (Raphael, 1965), but it conflicted with several others which reported either a direct or inverse relationship between organizational size and political outcome (dependent variable). The conflict between the present finding and other studies was explained in Chapter 4 as possibly being due to two reasons.

First, most studies employed different measures in assessing what they call "democracy." Differing operational definitions could very well have accounted for the different findings, e.g., if one study focused on the degree of opposition directed toward incumbents, a second on membership participation in convention caucuses, a third on leadership turnover, and a fourth on still another variable, then it would not be too difficult to see why different findings are reported relative to size of organization and its relationship to "democracy." Second, *most other investigations that cited a relationship between size of organization and "democracy" or "oligarchy" have failed to control for organizational age.* And since age and size of organization often are directly related, it is possible that organizational age may have influenced given organizational leadership to be oligarchic or non-oligarchic rather than size as has been theorized and reported in a number of studies.

In controlling for geographic environment, it was found that leadership turnover rates are essentially the same whether the organizations are in an industrial or agricultural area. This finding suggests industrial and bureaucratic values have little or no effect on oligarchic outcome in fraternal societies, or that the industrial influence is so widespread and pervasive now that non-industrial regions are no longer a vital factor (assuming they once were) in affecting the presence or absence of oligarchy.

The relationship between organizational complexity and oligarchy was also tested in the present inquiry. The findings, contrary to expectations, indicated that the less-complex associations were more oligarchic than were the complex organizations. This finding was explained on the basis of greater membership concern and interest likely to be present in complex organizations. This argument seems especially plausible in the light of the operational definition (number of convention reports and resolutions) employed in measuring complexity. Thus, complex organizations with relatively numerous reports and resolutions probably generate conflict and opposition which result in greater membership interest (Rose, 1955, pp. 159-163). This phenomenon may also stimulate a greater desire among the members for holding office and being a part of the leadership structure of their organization.

Contrary to what Raphael found regarding the relationship between organizations with spatially dispersed members and oligarchic outcome, the present study found that organizations with spatially dispersed members were less oligarchic than those which had a spatially concentrated membership. Since the method of operationalizing spatial distribution of members in the current inquiry was essentially the same as the one employed by Raphael, the different results in the two investigations might be due to different levels of aggregation. Raphael's study focused on *local* unions, while the fraternal orders were studied on the *state* level.

While the present investigation did not find any relationship between spatial distribution of members and organizational age, it did find a relationship between organizational size and spatial distribution of members. Organizations with spatially dispersed members were significantly larger in size. Finally, it was found that organizational complexity and spatial distribution of members are related, i.e., associations with spatially dispersed members are more complex than their counterparts.

At the outset of the inquiry, it was expected that expressive voluntary associations, specifically fraternal organizations, would not be immune to Michels' iron law of oligarchy. The data collected from 16 statewide fraternal organizations do indeed support the initial expectation. Thus, Michels' generalization, "Who says organization, says oligarchy," applies, not only to instrumental organizations, but also to expressive groups such as fraternal orders.

Since Lipset, Trow, and Coleman's study *Union Democracy* (1956) has been so widely cited as being an exception to Michels' law, it seems appropriate to discuss some of the findings in *Union Democracy* relative to the data in the present research which supports Michels' basic thesis.

Both the present study and *Union Democracy* employ the same dependent variable (leadership turnover) in assessing the degree of oligarchy. The emphasis on leadership turnover is found throughout the typographical union study. In fact, the characteristics which the authors cite as fostering democracy in the ITU such as the two-party system, constitutional statements limiting tenure of office, institutionalized opposition to the incumbent leaders, and retaining status and respect even after a leader is not returned to office have no real meaning apart from leadership turnover. These latter elements all contribute to turnover, or to what the authors call the institutionalized "practice of gracefully giving up office . . . ." (Lipset, Trow, and Coleman, 1956, p. 446).

Thus the different findings between *Union Democracy* and the present research might very well be due to methodological procedure. First, the authors of *Union Democracy* did not consider organizational age. Had they considered this variable their results might well have been different. This conclusion is not mere speculation but is implicitly suggested by Lipset. Trow, and Coleman. Without furnishing or discussing any figures, they note: "A much larger portion of the membership have held chapel office [political unit in a union shop] in the past," (1956, p. 201).

Second, *Union Democracy* makes much of the fact that a local union "law prescribes that no chapel chairman may hold office for more than two consecutive one-year terms, except with the unanimous consent of the members of his chapel" (1956, pp. 201-202). This practice, it must be noted, does not necessarily indicate a high turnover rate of leaders within the overall leadership structure. A chairman may relinquish his post and still remain in the leadership structure by obtaining a position on a committee. This was, in fact, true for every fraternal order in the present sample. The grand master (chairman) of each grand (state) lodge was usually limited to a one-year term of office; however, it was indeed rare *not* to find ex-grand masters holding other offices in the organization of which they once had been grand master. For example, former grand masters were almost always appointed to some important committee such as the Appeals Committee, the Jurisprudence Committee, the Charters and Dispensations Committee, or to the Board of Trustees. Moreover, most grand masters, as well as other executive officers, usually held committee posts prior to their election as executive officers. Had Lipset, Trow, and Coleman studied leadership turnover on committees, in addition to the executive level, they might have found that rules specifying short tenure for one position, do not necessarily preclude participation in leadership roles in other organizational posts.

Third, the authors of *Union Democracy* make frequent reference to the "high rate of turnover in office," but surprisingly fail to cite any turnover rates. Their failure to do so raises at least two questions: 1) What constitutes a "high" rate of turnover? 2) Relative to what other data does the ITU have a "high" turnover? The former question is important since no one, to the author's knowledge, has theoretically defined what constitutes a "low" or "high" leadership turnover. The latter question is significant in that comparative turnover rates are required, even if the ITU rates had been calculated. Consequently to say that the ITU has a "high rate of turnover in office" without offering comparative rates is rather meaningless. In contrast, the present volume provides comparative turnover rates by examining data from the first ten and most recent ten years of the organizations studied. This method not only copes with the problem of what is a "high" or "low" turnover in office, but it also provides a longitudinal perspective that is lacking in the literature.

In brief, the argument that the ITU constitutes a "deviant case" would be more convincing, if: 1) a longitudinal design had been employed which permitted intra-organizational comparison; 2) organizational age had been considered; 3) committee membership turnover had been examined; 4) turnover rates had been listed.

In addition to the methodological aspects employed in *Union Democracy,* brief mention might be made regarding the authors' conception of "democracy." The ITU is very much seen as being democratic because it has a two-party political structure.

An undue emphasis upon the two-party system could lead to some erroneous conclusions. For instance, given the presence of a two-party system in a given organization, it is conceivable to conclude *a priori* that the organization is non-oligarchic. The effect that such an attempt(s) would have on empirical research need not be stated.

Referring to Western Europe, the United States, and Canada (where two parties and multi-parties abound), Handman says the political systems in these countries "should be more properly described as parliamentary oligarchy shading off into oligarchical dictatorship, rather than parliamentary democracy" (Handman, 1933, p. 309). Griffith (1959) also believes that a two-party system does not necessarily lead to greater democracy. Moreover, it might be argued that parties may contend for sectional and private interests, rather than for the public or general membership interest. Apparently this is what Michels meant by saying: *die Führer weichen niemals der 'Masse' sondern immer nur anderen, neuen, Führern"* (Michels, 1928, p. 295).

Another conclusion might be that an organization is oligarchic unless it has an institutionalized two-party system. The data in the present study show that such an assumption is not necessarily true. Quite apart from any two-party system, it was found that organizational age was an important variable in affecting oligarchic outcome; fraternal organizations were significantly less oligarchic during their early years of existence than during their later years.

Turning to other studies, there is still another problem that merits attention. This pertains to the way democracy has been operationally defined. Chapter 4 referred to some of the diverse findings relative to organizational size and "democracy" reported in the literature. It was noted that the different findings, in part, might be attributed to the measure employed to ascertain the presence or absence of "democracy." For example, it is not uncommon to find studies utilizing only *one* or *two* of the following components: membership attendance, leadership turnover, policy-making participation of regular members, opposition to incumbents, and convention caucuses, etc. Obviously one or two components cannot be construed as having tapped democracy holistically. Yet, some authors who focused on one or two elements have discussed their findings as though they had incorporated every important component of democracy.

This practice probably betrays a democratic bias on the part of the individuals concerned.[1] Greater accuracy would be conveyed if the term democracy were employed more critically, for, as one writer said, democracy "is an abstraction—and it's

---

[1]Gray (1968) recently said that certain sociologists "speak more warmly" about given phenomena. Thus, the uncritical use of the term "democracy" might be accounted for in the light of some researchers having a greater affinity toward democracy.

likely to mean different things to different people" (Samstag, 1955, p. 95).

The present study did not employ the term democracy in discussing the data pertaining to fraternal associations. Instead expressions like "less oligarchic" or "higher leadership turn-over" were used. By not employing the word democracy in contrast to oligarchy the erroneous impression of seeing these two types of political phenomena as polar opposites was avoided.[2]

In conclusion several possibilities for further research suggest themselves on the basis of the present study. However, before these are stated the words of one political scientist seem appropriate. He said that very "little empirical research has been done in the field of political sociology either in defining Michels' underlying assumptions or even testing the validity of his thesis" (Neumann, 1956, p. 406). This observation is especially true regarding the relationship between organizational age and the formation of an oligarchic leadership. As mentioned earlier, research concerned with the iron law of oligarchy has virtually ignored the variable of organizational age. Most investigations have examined oligarchic outcome in the light of organizational size and overlooked the effects of organizational age.[3]

Thus, future research would do well if it studied, especially by means of longitudinal data, the effects of organizational age relative to oligarchic tendencies. In this regard it would be profitable if expressive organizations of a non-fraternal nature

---

[2]The contrast between oligarchy and democracy is evident throughout Michels' *Political Parties*. Lipset, Trow, and Coleman follow that same practice in *Union Democracy*. Others could be cited as well. Yet, it must be stated that Michels apparently did not wish to convey the idea that oligarchy was the polar opposite to democracy. At least on one occasion (1959, p. 168) he refers to a dictatorship arising out of an oligarchy, thereby saying that dictatorship or totalitarianism is a more extreme form of political structure. May, in agreement with Michels, says that oligarchy is "not the antithesis of democracy . . . ." (1965, p. 419). De Gré (1946) also does not see oligarchy as a polar to democracy.

[3]The studies by Raphael (1965) and Marcus (1966) are exceptions, but neither one of these is *exclusively* concerned with Michels' model. Both of these published articles are part of two broader focuses (Ph.D. studies) which did not have as their principal objective the study of oligarchic outcome. See Raphael (1963) and Marcus (1962).

were examined, particularly since the present study dealt with fraternal groups.

Another problem that needs further attention is the matter of different levels of aggregation. The paucity of data from various levels (local, state, and national) is very apparent in studies that deal with Michels' law. Additional data would not only enable important comparisons, but they would also give some indication whether generalizations might be reliably made from one level of aggregation to another regarding the presence or absence of oligarchy. For instance, is Michels' generalization, "Who says organization, says oligarchy," true for all levels of aggregation? Hopefully additional research will shed more light on this problem.

Finally, the fact that fraternal associations with spatially dispersed memberships were less oligarchic than were those with spatially concentrated memberships needs further examination, particularly since Raphael found the opposite to be true with union locals. The difference between the two studies might be due to the scope of measurement. The present research dichotomized a rather wide range of chapters (spatially concentrated membership: 12 to 46; spatially dispersed memberships: 104 to 272) per grand lodge, while Raphael divided a relatively narrow range of plant organizations (spatially concentrated memberships: one to five; spatially dispersed memberships: ten or more) per local union. In addition, the different levels of aggregation also might be considered in attempting to account for the difference between Raphael's study and the present one.

Hopefully these issues, together with some others raised in the present study, will be systematically examined in future research. Only then will Michels' iron law of oligarchy, so frequently cited, be more clearly understood.

BIBLIOGRAPHY

Acker, Julius W.
    1959   *Strange Altars.* St. Louis: Concordia Publishing House.
Alinsky, Saul D.
    1946   *Reveille for Radicals.* Chicago: The University of Chicago Press.
Anderson, Theodore R., and Seymour Warkov.
    1961   "Organizational Size and Functional Complexity: A Study of Administration in Hospitals," *American Sociological Review,* 26 (February): 23-28. 23-28.
Babchuk, Nicholas, and W.J. Goode.
    1951   "Work Incentives in a Self-determined Group," *American Sociological Review,* 16 (October): 679-687.
Barber, Bernard.
    1948   " 'Mass Apathy' and Voluntary Social Participation in the United States." Unpublished Ph.D. dissertation, Harvard University.
Barber, Bernard.
    1965   "Participation and Mass Apathy in Associations," *Leadership Studies.* Edited by Alvin W. Gouldner. Glencoe: The Free Press, 477-504.
Barker, Ernest (trans.)
    1946   *The Politics of Aristotle.* Oxford: The Clarendon Press.
Bell, F.A.
    1956   *Order of the Eastern Star.* Chicago: Ezra A. Cook Publications.
Bendix, Reinhard.
    1947   "Bureaucracy: The Problem and Its Setting," *American Sociological Review,* 12 (October): 493-507.
Blau, Peter M.
    1955   *The Dynamics of Bureaucracy.* Chicago: The University of Chicago Press.
Blau, Peter M.
    1956   *Bureaucracy in Modern Society.* New York: Random House.

Boneau, C. Alan.
  1960 "The Effects of Violation of Assumptions Under-
    lying the *t* Test," *Psychological Bulletin,* 57:
    49-64.

Brogan, D. W.
  1954 *Politics in America.* New York: Harper and
    Brothers.

Brown, Julia S.
  1956 "Union Size as a Function of Intra-Union Con-
    flict," *Human Relations,* 9: 75-89.

Burnham, James.
  1941 *The Managerial Revolution.* New York: The John
    Day Company.

Caplow, Theodore.
  1957 "Organizational Size," *Administrative Science
    Quarterly,* 1: 484-505.

Cass, Donn A.
  1957 *Negro Freemasonry and Segregation.* Chicago:.
    Ezra A. Cook Publication, Inc.

Cassinelli, C.W.
  1953 "The Law of Oligarchy," *American Political
    Science Review,* 47 (September): 773-784.

Chapin, F. Stuart.
  1951 "The Growth of Bureaucracy: An Hypothesis,"
    American Sociological Review, 16 (December):
    835-836.

Chapin, F. Stuart and John E. Tsouderos.
  1955 "Formalization Observed in Ten Voluntary
    Associations," *Social Forces,* 33 (May): 301-309.

Chapman, Alfred F.
  1892 "The Capitular Degrees," *History of the Ancient
    and Honorable Fraternity of Free and Accepted
    Masons.* Edited by Henry L. Stillson and William
    J. Hughan. Boston: The Fraternity Press,
    553-568.

Coil, Henry Wilson.
  1954 *A Comprehensive View of Freemasonry.* New
    York: Macoy Publishing and Masonic Supply
    Company.

Cole, Fay-Cooper, and Harris Gaylord Warren (eds.)
>   1955   *An Illustrated Outline History of Mankind.* Chicago: Spencer Press, Inc.

Coleman, James.
>   1956   "The Compulsive Pressures of Democracy in Unionism," *American Journal of Sociology,* 61 (May): 519-526.

Comptons Pictured Encyclopedia and Fact-Index.
>   1966   "Connecticut—State of Many Industries," III:
>   ed.   519-535; "Nebraska—Land of Fertile Prairies," X: 107-122.

Corry, J.A.
>   1947   *Elements of Democratic Government.* New York: Oxford University Press.

Craig, John G., and Edward Gross.
>   1970   "The Forum Theory of Organizational Democracy: Structural Guarantees as Time-Related Variable," *American Sociological Review,* 35 (February): 19-33.

Dalton, Melville.
>   1959   *Men Who Manage.* New York: John Wiley and Sons.

Darrah, Delmar Duane.
>   1967   *History and Evolution of Freemasonry.* Chicago: The Charles T. Powner Company.

Davis, Harry E.
>   1946   *A History of Freemasonry Among Negroes in America.* Published by the Supreme Council, Ancient and Accepted Scottish Rite of Freemasonry, Northern Jurisdiction, U.S.A., Prince Hall Affiliation.

Davis, James A., Joe L. Spaeth, and Carolyn Huson.
>   1961   "A Technique for Analyzing the Effects of Group Composition," *American Sociological Review,* 26 (April): 215-225.

Dean, Dwight G.
>   1960   "Alienation and Political Apathy," *Social Forces,* 38 (March): 185-189.

De Gré, Gerard.
>   1946   "Freedom and Social Structure," *American Sociological Review,* 11 (October): 529-536.

Dumas, John M.
1947 "Apathy-Our Fifth Column," *National Municipal Review,* 36 (October): 494-496, 502.
Duncan, Malcom C.
1968 *Masonic Ritual and Monitor.* Chicago: Ezra A. Cook Publications.
Durkheim, Emile.
1952 *Division of Labor in Society.* Glencoe: The Free Press.
Duverger, M.
1954 *Political Parties.* London: Methuen and Company.
Easton, David.
1956 *The Political System.* New York: Alfred A. Knopf.
Edelstein, J. David.
1965 "Democracy in a National Union: The British AEU," *Industrial Relations,* 4 (May): 105-125.
Etzioni, Amitai (ed.)
1961 *Complex Organizations: A Sociological Reader.* New York: Holt, Rinehart, and Winston.
Etzioni, Amitai.
1960 "Two Approaches to Organizational Analysis: A Critique and a Suggestion," *Administrative Science Quarterly,* (September): 257-278.
Faunce, Wm. A.
1962 "Size of Locals and Union Democracy," *American Journal of Sociology,* 68 (November): 291-298.
Fehrenbach, T. F.
1967 *Elkdom U.S.A.* Published by the Benevolent and Protective Order of Elks.
Finney, Charles G.
1948 *Character and Claims of Freemasonry.* Chicago: National Christian Association.
Foster, William Z.
1927 *Misleaders of Labor.* Chicago: Trade Union Educational League.
Garceau, Oliver.
1941 *The Political Life of the American Medical Association.* Cambridge: Harvard University Press.

Gist, Noel P.
1940   "Secret Societies: A Cultural Study of Frater-
nalism in the United States," *The University of
Missouri Studies,* 15 (October): 9-176.

Gist, Noel P.
1943   "Fraternal Societies," *Development of Collective
Enterprise.* Edited by Seba Eldridge. Lawrence,
Kansas: The University of Kansas Press.

Gordon, C. Wayne, and Nicholas Babchuk.
1959   "A Typology of Voluntary Associations," *American Sociological Review,* 24 (February): 22-29.

Gouldner, Alvin W.
1955   "Methaphysical Pathos and the Theory of Bureaucracy," *American Political Science Review,* 49
(June): 496-507.

Gray, David J.
1968   "Value-free Sociology: A Doctrine of Hypocrisy
and Irresponsibility," *Sociological Quarterly,* 9
(Spring): 176-185.

Griffith, Ernest S.
1959   *Congress: Its Contemporary Role,* New York:
New York University Press.

Grusky, Oscar.
1961   "Corporate Size, Bureaucratization and Managerial Succession," *American Journal of Sociology,* 67 (November): 261-269.

Gusfield, Joseph R.
1955   "Social Structure and Moral Reform: A Study of
the Women's Christian Temperance Union,"
American Journal of Sociology, 61 (November):
221-232.

Hage, Jerald.
1965   "An Axiomatic Theory of Organizations," *Administrative Science Quarterly,* 10 (December):
289-320.

Haire, Mason.
1959   *Modern Organization Theory.* New York: John
Wiley and Sons.

Hall, Richard, J. Eugene Haas, and Norman J. Johnson.
    1967   "Organizational Size, Complexity, and Formaliza-
            tion," *American Sociological Review,* 32 (Decem-
            ber): 903-912.
Handman, Max.
    1933   "The Bureaucratic Culture Pattern and Political
            Revolution," *American Journal of Sociology,* 39
            (November): 301-313.
Hannah, Walton.
    1952   *Darkness Visible.* London: Augustine Press.
Hannah, Walton.
    1954   *Christian by Degrees.* London: Augustine Press.
Harrison, Paul M.
    1959   *Authority and Power in the Free Church Tradi-
            tion.* Princeton: Princeton University Press.
Hawley, Amos H., Walter Boland, and Margaret Boland.
    1965   "Population Size and Administration in Institu-
            tions of Higher Education," *American Sociologi-
            cal Review,* 30 (April): 252-255.
Hemphill, J. K.
    1950   "Relations Between the Size of the Group and
            the Behavior of 'Superior' Leaders," *Journal of
            Social Psychology,* 32 (August): 11-22.
Herberg, Will.
    1943   "Bureaucracy and Democracy in Labor Unions,"
            Antioch Review, 3 (Fall): 405-417.
Hicks, John D.
    1931   *The Populist Revolt.* Minneapolis: University of
            Minnesota Press.
Hook, Sidney.
    1943   *The Hero in History,* New York: The John Day
            Company.
The International Odd Fellow.
    1943   "History of Odd Fellowship," (March): 7,
Jacoby, Arthur P., and Nicholas Babchuk.
    1963   "Instrumental and Expressive Voluntary Associa-
            tions," *Sociology and Social Research,* 47 (July):
            461-471.

Jacoby, Arthur P.
    1965   "Some Correlates of Instrumental and Expressive
            Orientations   to   Associational   Membership,"
            Sociological Inquiry, 35 (Spring): 163-175.
Jayne-Weaver, Ida M., and Emma D. Wood.
    1925   *History of the Order of Pythian Sisters.* Seattle:
            Peters Publishing Company.
Jones, Bernard E.
    1950   *Freemasons' Guide and Compendium.* New York:
            Macoy Publishing and Masonic Supply Company.
Kibbe, P. C.
    1930   *Damon and Pythias.* Tenino, Washington: Inde-
            pendent Publishing Company.
King, C. Harold.
    1956   *A History of Civilization.* New York: Scribner's
            Sons.
King, C. Wendell.
    1956   *Social Movements in the United States.* New
            York: Random House.
Klapp, Orin E.
    1964   *Symbolic Leaders.* Chicago: Aldine Publishing
            Company.
Klapp, Orin E.
    1969   *Collective Search for Identity.* New York: Holt,
            Rinehart, and Winston, Inc.
Knoop, Douglas and G. P. Jones.
    1949   *The Medieval Mason.* Manchester: Manchester
            University Press.
Kopald, Sylvia.
    1924   *Rebellion in Labor Unions.* New York: Boni and
            Liveright.
Kovner, Joseph, and Herbert J. Lahne.
    1953   "Shop Society and the Union," *Industrial and
            Labor Relations Review,* 7 (October): 3-14.
Krueger, Cynthia.
    1968   "Prairie Protest: The Medicare Conflict in
            Saskatchewan," *Agrarian Socialism.* Edited by
            Seymour M. Lipset. Garden City, New York:
            Anchor Books, 405-434.

Lasswell, Harold D., Daniel Lerner, and Easton C. Rothwell.
1952 *The Comparative Study of Elite.* The Hoover Institute and Library on War, Revolution, and Peace. Stanford, California: Stanford University Press.

Latourette, Kenneth Scott.
1953 *A History of Christianity.* New York: Harper and Brothers.

Lazarsfeld, Paul F., and H. Menzel.
1961 "On the Relation Between Individual and Collective Properties," *Complex Organizations: A Sociological Reader.* Edited by Amitai Etzioni. New York: Holt, Rinehart and Winston, 422-440.

Life.
1956 "Busy Brotherly World of Freemasonry," 41 (October 8): 104-112, 115-118, 120, 122.

Lipset, Seymour M.
1954 "The Political Process in Trade Unions: A Theoretical Statement," *Freedom and Control in Modern Society.* Edited by Monroe Berger, Theodore Abel and Charles H. Page. New York: Van Nostrand, 82-124.

Lipset, Seymour M., Martin Trow, and James Coleman.
1956 *Union Democracy.* Garden City, New York: Doubleday Company, Inc.

Lipset, Seymour M.
1960 *The Political Man.* Garden City, New Jersey: Doubleday and Company.

MacIver, Robert M.
1947 *The Web of Government.* New York: The Macmillan Company.

Mackey, Albert G.
1946 *Encyclopedia of Freemasonry.* Chicago: The Masonic History Company.

Mackey, Albert G.
1967 *Jurisprudence of Freemasonry.* Chicago: The Charles T. Powner Company.

Marcus, Philip.
1962 "Trade Union Structure: A Study in Formal Organization." Unpublished Ph.D. dissertation, The University of Chicago.

Marcus, Philip.
1966 "Union Conventions and Executive Boards: A Formal Analysis of Organizational Structure," *American Sociological Review,* 31 (February): 61-70.

May, John D.
1965 "Democracy, Organization, Michels," *American Political Science Review,* 59 (June): 417-429.

Merz, Charles.
1927 "Sweet Land of Secrecy," *Harper's Monthly Magazine,* CLIV: 329-334.

Michels, Robert.
1911 *Zur Soziologie Des Parteiwesens In Der Modernen Demokratie: Untersuchungen Ueber Die Oligarchischen Tendenzen Des Gruppenlebens.* Leipzig: Verlag von Dr. Werner Klinkhardt.

Michels, Robert.
1928 "Grundsätzliches zum Problem der Demokratie," *Zeitschrift für Politik,* 17: 289-295.

Michels, Robert.
1959 *Political Parties: A Sociological Study of the Oligarchical Tendencies of Modern Democracy.* New York: Dover Publications, Inc.

Miller, Daniel R., and Guy E. Swanson.
1958 *The Changing American Parent: A Study in the Detroit Area.* New York: John Wiley and Sons.

Mosca, Gaetano.
1939 *The Ruling Class.* New York: McGraw-Hill Book Company.

Neuman, Sigmund.
1956 "Toward a Comparative Study of Political Parties," *Modern Political Parties: Approaches to Political Parties.* Edited by Sigmund Neumann. Chicago: The University of Chicago Press, 395-421.

Pareto, Vilfredo.
　　1935　*The Mind and Society.* Edited by Arthur Living-
　　　　ston. 4 Volumes, New York: Harcourt, Brace and
　　　　Company.
Parker, Thomas W.
　　1963　*The Knights Templar in England.* Tuscon: Uni-
　　　　versity of Arizona Press.
Parsons, Talcott.
　　1949　*Essays in Sociological Theory.* Glencoe: The Free
　　　　Press.
Parson, Talcott.
　　1951　*The Social System.* Glencoe: The Free Press.
Pike, Albert.
　　1881　*Morals and Dogma of the Ancient and Accepted
　　　　Scottish Rite of Freemasonry.* Charleston, South
　　　　Carolina: Supreme Council of the 33rd Degree for
　　　　the Southern Jurisdiction of the United States.
Plato.
　　1935　*The Republic.* Trans. Paul Shorey. Cambridge,
　　　　Massachusetts: Harvard University Press.
Pollack, Norman.
　　1962　*The Populist Response to Industrial America.*
　　　　Cambridge, Massachusetts: Harvard University
　　　　Press.
Presthus, Robert.
　　1962　*The Organizational Society.* New York: Vintage
　　　　Books.
Prewitt, Kenneth.
　　1970　"Political Ambitions, Volunteerism, and Electoral
　　　　Accountability," *American Political Science Re-
　　　　view,* 64 (March): 5-17.
Raphael, Edna E.
　　1963　"Welfare Activity in the Local Union: A Study in
　　　　the Sampling of Organizations." Unpublished
　　　　Ph.D. dissertation, The University of Chicago.
Raphael, Edna E.
　　1965　"Power Structure and Membership Dispersion in
　　　　Unions," *American Journal of Sociology,* 61
　　　　(November): 274-283.

Richardson, Jabez.
    n.d. *Monitor of Freemasonry.* Philadelphia: David McKay Publisher.
Riesman, David, and Nathan Glazer.
    1965 "Criteria for Political Apathy," *Leadership Studies.* Edited by Alvin W. Gouldner. Glencoe: The Free Press, 505-559.
Ronayne, Edmond.
    1959 *Handbook of Freemasonry.* Chicago: Ezra A. Cook Publication.
Rose, Arnold.
    1954 *Theory and Method in the Social Sciences.* Minneapolis: The University of Minnesota.
Rose, Arnold.
    1955 "Voluntary Associations-Competition and Conflict," *Social Forces,* 34 (December): 159-163.
Rose, Arnold.
    1967 *The Power Structure: Political Processes in American Society.* New York: Oxford University Press.
Roy, D. F.
    1952 "Quota Restriction and Goldbricking in a Machine Shop," *American Journal of Sociology,* 57 (March): 427-442.
Samstag, Nicholas.
    1955 "Strategy," *The Engineering of Consent.* Edited by Edward L. Bernays. Norman, Oklahoma: University of Oklahoma Press, 94-137.
Schmidt, Alvin J., and Nicholas Babchuk.
    1972 "Formal Voluntary Associations and Change Over Time: A Study of American Fraternal Associations." *Journal of Voluntary Action Research,* 1 (Winter): 46-55.
Schumpeter, Joseph A.
    1942 *Capitalism, Socialism, and Democracy.* New York: Harper & Row.
Scott, W. Richard.
    1964 "Organization Theory," *Handbook of Modern Sociology.* Edited by R. L. Faris. Chicago: Rand McNally and Company, 485-529.

Seidman, Joel.
1953 "Democracy in Labor Unions," *Journal of Political Economy,* 61 (June): 221-231.

Seidman, Joel, *et al.*
1958 *The Worker Views His Union.* Chicago: The University of Chicago Press.

Selznick, Philip.
1949 *TVA and the Grass Roots.* Berkeley and Los Angeles: University of California Press.

Selznick, Philip.
1950 "The Iron Law of Bureaucracy," *Modern Review,* (January): 157-165.

Sills, David L.
1968 "Voluntary Associations: Sociological Aspects," *International Encyclopedia of the Social Sciences.* Edited by David L. Sills. New York: The Macmillan Company and The Free Press, 362-379.

Simmel, Georg.
1906 "The Sociology of Secrecy and of Secret Societies," *American Journal of Sociology,* 11 (January): 441-498.

Sims, Mary S.
1939 *The Natural History of a Social Institution-The Y.W.C.A.* New York: The Women's Press.

Speed, Frederic.
1892 "Knights Templar and Allied Orders," *History of the Ancient and Honorable Fraternity of Free and Accepted Masons.* Edited by Henry L. Stillson and William J. Hughan. Boston: The Fraternity Publishing Company, 699-730.

Spinard, William.
1960 "Correlates of Trade Union Participation: A Summary of the Literature," *American Sociological Review,* 25 (April): 237-244.

Stevens, Albert C.
1907 *Cyclopedia of Fraternities.* New York: E. G. Treat.

Stillson, Henry J.
  1892 "The Documentary Early History of the Frater-
         nity," *History of the Ancient and Honorable
         Fraternity of Free and Accepted Masons.* Edited
         by Henry L. Stillson and William J. Hughan.
         Boston: The Fraternity Publishing Company,
         167-178.

Strauss, George.
  1956 "Control by the Membership in Building Trade
         Unions," *American Journal of Sociology,* 61
         (May): 527-535.

Strauss, George, and Leonard P. Sayles.
  1953 "The Local Union Meeting," *Industrial and Labor
         Relations Review,* 6 (June): 238-258.

Tannenbaum, Arnold S., and Robert L. Kahn.
  1958 *Participation in Union Locals.* Evanston: Row,
         Peterson.

Terrien, Frederic W., and Donald L. Mills.
  1955 "The Effect of Changing Size Upon the Internal
         Structure of Organizations," *American Sociologi-
         cal Review,* 20 (February): 11-13.

Toch, Hans.
  1965 *The Social Psychology of Social Movements.*
         Indianapolis: The Bobbs-Merrill Company.

Treece, Henry.
  1962 *The Crusaders.* New York: Mentor Books.

Truman, David.
  1951 *The Governmental Process.* New York: Alfred A.
         Knopf.

Tsouderos, John E.
  1955 "Organizational Change in Terms of a Series of
         Selected Variables," *American Sociological Re-
         view,* 20 (April): 206-210.

Udy, Stanley H. Jr.
  1959 "The Structure of Authority in Non-Industrial
         Production Organizations," *American Journal of
         Sociology,* 64 (May): 582-584.

Van Valkenberg, Jon.
    1887 *The Knights of Pythias Complete Manual and Textbook.* Canton, Ohio: Memento Publishing Company.

Wanner, William.
    1964 *Fraternal Review.* A Report Prepared for the Masonic Grand Lodge of Nebraska.

Warner, W. Lloyd.
    1949 *Democracy in Jonesville.* New York: Harper and Row.

Weber, Max.
    1946 "The Protestant Sects and the Spirit of Capitalism," *From Max Weber.* Edited by H. H. Gerth and C. Wright Mills. New York: Oxford University Press, 302-322.

Weber, Max.
    1947 *The Theory of Social and Economic Organizations.* Translated by Talcott Parsons and A. M. Henderson. Glencoe: The Free Press.

Wedgwood, Camilla H.
    1930 "The Nature and Functions of Secret Societies," *Oceania,* 1 (July): 129-145.

Wells, Alan F.
    1967 "Fraternal Organizations: Great Britain History," ed. *Encyclopaedia Britannica,* IX: 812-814.

Whalen, William J.
    1966 *Handbook of Secret Organizations.* Milwaukee: Bruce Publishing Company.

Whyte, William H.
    1957 *The Organization Man.* New York: Anchor Books.

Wright, Louis B.
    1963 *The Democratic Experience.* Chicago: Scott. Foresman and Company.

Young, Michael.
    1958 *The Rise of the Meritocracy.* Baltimore: Penguin Books, Ltd.

Zelditch, Morris Jr., and Terrence K. Hopkins.
1961 "Laboratory Experiments with Organizations,"
Complex Organizations: A Sociological Reader.
Edited by Amitai Etzioni. New York: Holt,
Rinehart and Winston, 464-484.

SPECIAL

FRATERNAL BIBLIOGRAPHY

Annual Convention Proceedings of the Kansas Elks Association.
1907-16; 1960-69.
Brief History of the Knights of Pythias. Supreme Lodge
Extension and Educational Commission. [n.d].
*Constitution and Statues, Benevolent and Protective Order of
Elks.* Published by the authority of the Grand Lodge.
1968-69 ed.
*Convention Programs, Order of Pythian Sisters: Grand Temple
of Nebraska.* 1930-39; 1959-68
Grand Lodge Bulletin, Iowa, June, 1969.
*Journal of Proceedings of the Grand Lodge, Independent Order
of Odd Fellows of Nebraska.* 1858-67; 1958-68.
*Journal of Proceedings of International Association of Rebekah
Assemblies.* 1958-67.
*Journal of Proceedings of the Right Worthy Grand Lodge of the
United States of America and the Sovereign Grand
Lodge of the Independent Order of Odd Fellows.*
Volume I. 1852.
Journal of Proceedings of Supreme Lodge of Knights of Pythias,
1870; 1875.
List of Masonic Lodges. Bloomington, Illinois: Pantagraph
Printing and Stationary Company. 1968.
Masonic Service Association. *An Introduction to the Problems
of Declining Memberships and Poor Attendance.*
Washington, D.C., 1960.

Masonic Service Association. *One Hundred One Questions About Freemasonry.* Washington, D.C. 1968.

Official Record of Proceedings of the Fifty-second Convention of Supreme Lodge, Knights of Pythias. 1964.

Proceedings Of the Grand Chapter of Connecticut, the Order of the Eastern Star. 1874-83; 1958-67.

Proceedings of the Grand Chapter of Nebraska, the Order of the Eastern Star. 1875-84; 1956-65.

Proceedings of the Grand Commandery of the Knights Templar of Connecticut. 1821-30; 1959-68.

Proceedings of the Grand Commandery of the Knights Templar of Nebraska. 1871-80; 1957-68.

Proceedings of the Grand Council of Royal and Select Masons of Connecticut. 1873-82; 1955-66.

Proceedings of the Grand Council of Royal and Select Masons of Nebraska. 1872-81; 1955-64.

Proceedings of the Grand Lodge of Connecticut, Ancient, Free, and Accepted Masons. 1789-98; 1958-67.

Proceedings of the Grand Lodge of Nebraska, Ancient, Free and Accepted Masons. 1857-66; 1958-67.

Proceedings of the Grand Lodge of the Benevolent and Protective Order of Elks. 1959-68.

Proceedings of Grand Lodge of Knights of Pythias of Nebraska. 1869-78; 1958-67.

Proceedings of Grand Lodge of Knights of Pythias of Vermont, 1896-1905; 1936-45.

Proceedings, Order of Pythian Sisters: Supreme Temple. 1925; 1968.

Proceedings of Rebekah Assembly, Independent Order of Odd Fellows of Nebraska. 1894-1903; 1955-64.

Proceedings of the Royal Arch Masons of Connecticut. 1806-16; 1955-64..

Revised, Illustrated Ritual for Subordinate Lodges of Knights of Pythias. Chicago: Ezra A. Cook. 1945.

Revised Odd-Fellowship Illustrated: The Complete Revised Ritual of the Lodge, Encampment and Rebekah Degrees. 1951.

Supreme Constitutions and Statutes and Grand and Subordinate Constitutions of Knights of Pythias. 1964.

INDEX OF NAMES